YOU ARE
THINKING OF
TEACHING?

SEYMOUR B. SARASON

YOU ARE THINKING OF TEACHING?

opportunities,

problems,

realities

JOSSEY-BASS PUBLISHERS
San Francisco, California

LB
1775
S325
1993

Substantial discounts on bulk quantities of Jossey-Bass books
are available to corporations, professional associations, and other
organizations. For details and discount information, contact the
special sales department at Jossey-Bass Inc., Publishers.
(415) 433-1740; Fax (415)433-0499.

For sales outside the United States, contact Maxwell Macmillan
International Publishing Group, 866 Third Avenue, New York,
New York 10022.

Manufactured in the United States of America

The paper used in this book is acid-free and meets the guidelines
for permanence and durability of the Committee on Production
Guidelines for Book Longevity of the Council on Library Resources.

Library of Congress Cataloging-in-Publication Data

Sarason, Seymour Bernard, date.
　　You are thinking of teaching? : Opportunities, problems, realities
　/ Seymour B. Sarason.
　　　p.　　　cm. — (The Jossey-Bass education series).
　　ISBN 1-55542-569-0
　　1. Teaching—Vocational guidance. 2. Education—Study and
teaching(Higher).　　I. Title.　　II. Series.
LB1775.S325　　1993
371.1'0023—dc20
　　　　　　　　　　　　　　　　　　　　　　　93-10694
　　　　　　　　　　　　　　　　　　　　　　　CIP

FIRST EDITION
HB Printing　　10 9 8 7 6 5 4 3 2 1　　　　　　*Code 9363*

The

Jossey-Bass

Education Series

To Nathaniel Lee Sarason Feuerstein
Born March 8, 1993

May you come to know the difference
between knowledge and wisdom

contents

preface

*t*he central theme in *The Case for Change: Rethinking the Preparation of Educators** is that reform efforts have emphasized repair over prevention. *Emphasize* is too weak a word. What I attempted to do was to indicate what it would or could mean if we took the preventive orientation seriously in preparing educators. Many factors converged to motivate me to write that book, not the least of which was the fact, and it was and is a fact, that preparatory programs were inadequate in alerting students to the realities of classrooms, schools, and school systems. It seemed obvious to me that unless these programs better prepared students for those realities, reform efforts could not be expected to be successful. Long before I wrote that book, I was tempted to write a book in which I would try to sensitize prospective teachers to what life would be like for the professional teacher. It would be a book on the theme of "forewarned is forearmed." If I did not write that

*Sarason, S. B. *The Case for Change: Rethinking the Preparation of Educators.* San Francisco: Jossey-Bass, 1993.

book, it was not for a lack of motivation or conviction. But as I wrote *The Case for Change*, I knew that I could and should no longer postpone writing that book, the contents of which have a long personal history. It was not an easy decision, for reasons I shall briefly discuss.

I resisted writing this book for fear that what I would say would be perceived as having an effect contrary to my intention—to portray to those considering a career in teaching a picture containing exciting opportunities to understand themselves, students, and our society. The source of my resistance was that those opportunities would be believable only if those contemplating a career in teaching knew the nature of the challenges they would confront. I long ago learned that too many people chose such a career abysmally unsophisticated about what they would be up against staying intellectually and professionally alive. Despite such a lack, some teachers had the courage and motivation to continue growing, learning, and changing. Too many teachers did not, and in saying that I intend no criticism whatsoever. The conditions for a productive, satisfying career require more than personal characteristics; they also require a social-intellectual-professional atmosphere in which those characteristics stand a chance to be expressed. What I found impressive were those instances where that atmosphere existed minimally or not at all but where individual teachers successfully sought to change that atmosphere. It took me too many years finally to "hear" what almost all teachers were telling me: "I wish I had been made more knowledgeable about and sensitive to the realities of teaching real kids in a real school. If I knew when I started a fraction of what I know now, I might or might not have chosen a career in teaching, but I would have reacted to the realities in a better way." One teacher articulated well something that for me had the clear, loud ring of truth: "It took me at least five years to overcome the tendency to regard myself as powerless to do anything to make my school an alive place. In my preparatory program, my instructors and supervisors—who were well-intentioned, sincere people—conveyed the impression that my major, even sole responsibility was to the students in my classroom. What was happening in the rest of the school was important *but none of my business* [her emphasis]. That, of course, was not true. When I had that insight, my whole outlook changed, and so did my role in the school. I helped change that school. I became a more happy teacher *and person* [her emphasis]. If I didn't feel all-powerful, I certainly didn't wallow in feelings of powerlessness. It wasn't easy, but it has paid off." That was said to me twenty-five years ago, long before the issue of the role of teachers in educational decision making gained currency. If it has gained currency, albeit far more on the level of rhetoric than in practice, the fact remains that today those who choose teaching as a career are inadequately sensitized to the problems they will confront and what *they* can and *should* do about them. That is a central theme in this book. It is a theme, a belief, that literally forced me to write this book. "Salvation" has its internal and external sources and conditions.

If I believe anything, it is that unless and until those who enter teaching have a better comprehension of what life as a teacher too frequently is, *and what it should and can be*, improving our schools is a doomed affair. Yes, other things have to happen, other changes have to be made. But unless teachers are better prepared to play a more active, even militant role in such changes, improvement will be minuscule. It is that belief that permits me to emphasize in this book that those who today choose teaching as a career are doing so at a time when, individually and as a group, they can make a difference. No career other than teaching allows one as much possibility of meeting and coping with a threefold challenge: better understanding of oneself, others (students, parents), *and the society in which we live.* This is not an easy challenge. It is not for the fainthearted or those who view *the* teacher in *a* classroom as a desirable (or possible) monastic existence. It is a challenge that when understood and realistically confronted guarantees excitement, frustration, and personal-intellectual-professional growth.

What I say in this book to those contemplating a career in teaching can be put this way: "You may perceive what I say as coming from a pessimist who says the bottle is half-empty. I hope you will see it as coming from someone who sees the bottle is half-full and believes that you can increase its contents."

I have made no effort to cover the waterfront of issues and problems about which a person contemplating a career in teaching should ponder. And precisely because I am writing for such people, I avoid—at least I have tried to avoid—jargon, references to studies, and statistics. I have restricted myself to the confines of a conversational style, and within those confines to what I think I have learned that may be helpful.

I will be more than gratified if this book has meaning for two other groups: those who are currently in a preparatory program and those who are their instructors or supervisors. If what I have written is seen by others as incomplete or misdirected or wrong in some ways, and stimulates them to write their own books, I will feel that my effort was not in vain.

Acknowledgments

It is fair to say that a large part of what I say in this book is no more and no less than what teachers have told me. Over the decades, I have had many long, fascinating, instructive, candid discussions with teachers. It was those discussions that forced on me a truth we apparently have to learn again and again and again throughout our lives: Don't ever confuse what teachers (any people) say they think and feel with what they think and feel in the quiet of their nights. If in the past I have been critical of what and how teachers teach their students, I am delighted to be able to say that teachers have taught me a great deal about teaching, teachers, and schools. I must single out two teachers, now my friends, who "instructed" me well. One is Ed Meyer, who at great personal cost, but not at the expense of dearly held values and intellectual integrity, has been a constructive and persistent critic of the preparation of teachers. The other is Robert Echter, who helped me understand how keenly teachers feel the lack of collegiality in their schools, a sense of community they passionately desire but were not helped to think about or to assume the obligation to achieve.

And, of course, I am again indebted to Lisa Pagliaro, who continues to be able to read my handwriting. Why and how she does so continue to mystify me. In any event, I thank God for big favors in the form of Ed Meyer, Bob Echter, and Lisa Pagliaro.

This book is homage to a man who was the dearest of friends and a great and influential educator, and who in countless ways focused my interest and attention on issues in the preparation and lives of teachers. Each of the late Burton Blatt's teachers-to-be knew the difference between passively accepting things as they are and the way they should and can be. And in knowing that difference, they also knew what their obligation was.

New Haven, Connecticut   Seymour B. Sarason
June 1993

the author

Seymour B. Sarason is professor of psychology emeritus in the Department of Psychology and at the Institution for Social and Policy Studies at Yale University. He founded, in 1962, and directed, until 1970, the Yale Psycho-Educational Clinic, one of the first research and training sites in community psychology. He received his Ph.D. degree from Clark University in 1942 and holds honorary doctorates from Syracuse University, Queens College, Rhode Island College, and Lewis and Clark College. He has received an award for distinguished contributions to the public interest and several awards from the divisions of clinical and community psychology of the American Psychological Association, as well as two awards from the American Association on Mental Deficiency.

Sarason is the author of numerous books and articles. His more recent books include *The Case for Change: Rethinking the Preparation of Educators* (1993), *Letters to an Educational President* (1993), *The Predictable Failure of Educational Reform: Can We Change Course Before It's Too Late?* (1990), *The Challenge of*

Art to Psychology (1990), and *The Making of an American Psychologist: An Autobiography* (1988). He has made contributions in such fields as mental retardation, culture and personality, projective techniques, teacher training, the school culture, and anxiety in children.

chapter 1

JUSTIFYING THIS BOOK

*t*his book is for those individuals contemplating a career in education. How does someone like me who has never taught in a public school justify writing such a book? The reader deserves that the question be answered, and I owe it to myself to try to convince the reader that what I say was not dreamed up in an armchair. That does not mean that you will or should agree with what I say but it does mean that you should not lightly dismiss points of view different from your own. We are all familiar with the quip that the two things we can count on in our lives are death and taxes. There is a third thing: in our past, present, and future, something we thought was "right" was or will be wrong. That is as true for me as for the reader. I say that as a way of indicating that this book reflects an agonizing review of what I have learned from my experiences, mistakes, and successes. In one or another way I have been connected with schools for almost fifty years, either as a clinical psychologist, a researcher in schools, a consultant, or an active participant in teacher training programs. And those have been years during which the society generally and schools in particular have undergone dramatic change, although one should never confuse change with progress. It was hard, I would say impossible, for anyone living through those decades to continue to think in accustomed ways. If it was true in those decades, it is still true today.

The immediate stimulus for this book is my bedrock belief that nothing will desirably change in our schools until those who enter teaching have a more realistic grasp of what life in a school is, can, and should be. It took me years to realize that those who were choosing teaching as a career did so more on the basis of fantasy than on reality-based expectations. That is understandable. After all, a person choosing a career in teaching is, relatively speaking, young, inexperienced, idealistic, unformed, and uninformed. There is truth to that, but I have had to conclude that it is a very partial truth, which obscures what can be with what is. No one can know all that one should know about choosing a particular career, but that is no excuse for not trying to help that person become aware, to some degree at least, of the problems one will predictably encounter in that career. And when I say "help," I mean not only providing information but alerting the person to a most fateful question: Is there a match between the obligations, responsibilities, and problems inherent in that career and the individual's personal style, needs, and goals? That is a question many professionals failed to struggle with at the point of making a career decision, with the consequence that they have some regret about the choice they make. That is as true for teachers as it is for lawyers, physicians, engineers, and businesspeople.

We are living at a time when there are scads of proposals to improve our schools. It is not the purpose of this book to examine these proposals. However widely and wildly these proposals differ, they rest on the assumption that those who enter teaching have a working grasp of what it means to live life in a school. On the basis of hundreds (perhaps thousands) of conversations and interactions with teachers, I can assure the reader that that assumption is wholly or in large measure invalid. This is not to say that most of these teachers regretted their choice of career, although some did, but rather that they wished that they had made the choice with more scrutiny, that someone had alerted them to what they later came to see as predictable problems a teacher will encounter. As one teacher said to me, "I do not regret having chosen teaching, but I do regret that I made the choice on grounds that guaranteed I would have a lot of personal and professional problems, not about my classroom but about my place in the school and school system." One teacher summed up what scores of teachers told me: "Before I became a teacher, I imagined that I would be part of a school family, that I would be part of an intimate, stimulating group of friends who shared experiences and had common goals. It hasn't worked out that way, but at least I know from teachers in other schools that I should not blame myself." Still another teacher, relatively new to teaching, articulated what I frequently heard from others: "When I decided to go into teaching, no one told me that my self-respect would force me to be assertive, even confronting about how decisions affecting me were made. Fortunately, I am no shrinking violet but, frankly, I didn't expect to have to be as forthright as I have become."

If what these teachers said does not paint the rosiest of pictures, the fact is that there are schools, by no means numerous, in which teachers feel worthy, respected, consulted, a sense of personal-intellectual collegiality, the sense that they belong.

And some of these schools are what are termed "ghetto" schools, where the appearance of physical decay, inadequate resources, and a slumlike surrounding masks the reality of a devoted, closely knit, energy-demanding, creative group of educators who would not want to be elsewhere. What is noteworthy about these schools is they are what they are in large part because teachers exercised initiative and leadership about matters beyond their classrooms. So when I say that little of the goals of reform efforts will be realized unless and until teachers are better prepared to understand, deal with, and change the quality of personal and intellectual life in schools, I am saying that those who contemplate a career in teaching have to examine who and what they are and want to become. Not everyone seeking a career in medicine or law or psychology has the personal and temperamental characteristics such a career requires, both practically and ideally. It is no different for those seeking to enter the profession of teaching.

It is a truism to say that each of us is literally a unique person. It is also a truism to say that each profession has its unique aspects: for example, where and how that profession is practiced, the responsibilities and obligations of such a professional, the demands on life-style such a profession makes, and the kinds of personal and intellectual problems that will predictably be encountered over a professional lifetime. If you conclude that teaching is not for you, that is no basis for self-criticism. Teaching is not for everyone. If you conclude that teaching is for you, it should be on the basis that *you* know who and what you are, the ways in which you will be challenged, and that you are prepared to be other than a silent, passive participant in the socially fateful and crucial effort to improve our schools; that is, the particular school or schools in which you work. It is unfair and unrealistic to expect teachers to change the society. It is not unfair or unrealistic to expect teachers to change, in part if not wholly, the conditions in which they and their students experience personal and intellectual growth. Teachers have brought about such changes. If the number of instances is smaller than we like, let us not gloss over the fact that some groups of teachers successfully departed from tradition and the results have been both exciting and gratifying, despite all sorts of frustration and uphill climbs. These teachers were truly not shrinking violets. They were not content to live their professional lives in an encapsulated classroom in an encapsulated school.

I said that the immediate stimulus for this book is my belief that little or nothing will desirably change in our schools unless or until those who enter teaching have a more realistic grasp of what life in a school is, can, and should be. In discussing that belief, I have also answered the question about how I, who have never taught in a public school, can justify writing a book for those thinking about teaching as a career. The answer is simple: what I say in this book is what teachers have told me. I do not want to give the impression that I met with teachers, I asked questions, and out came answers. It was not as simple as that. What I learned from teachers—and in this respect, they were my teachers—I got after I had spent time in their classroom and school, after they perceived me as someone interested in how they thought and felt as teachers, after they came to believe me when I said that teaching is (that is, can be) a wondrous combination of intellectual challenge, interpersonal sensitivity, superhuman patience, creativity, a healthy degree of frustration tolerance, and more. And some of these teachers had the courage and candor to say that they fell short of the mark.

There is one pervasive theme in this book that was rarely

verbalized by teachers and represents a conclusion to which I was forced. Simply put, it is that teachers vastly underestimate their power to change things. Teachers tend to see themselves at the bottom of the hierarchy of power in educational decision making. That is the way things are, although that is slowly changing. And yet what teachers were telling me *implied* that unless their sense of powerlessness changed, the effort to reform schools would be another instance of "the more things change, the more they remain the same." More than that, their basic stance was that alterations in their relationship to educational decision making would come from those higher in the hierarchy of power. That will not happen, in my opinion, except infrequently and (probably) begrudgingly. It will come primarily from teachers exercising initiative, leadership, and courage. That is why I regard who will choose teaching as a career to be so crucial in determining what will happen to our schools in the long- and short-term future.

I did not write this book to persuade or dissuade. I wrote it as a plea to those contemplating a teaching career that in making a decision they never lose sight of two questions: What should I seek to learn about what teaching involves intellectually, interpersonally, socially, developmentally? Am I the kind of person willing and able to enter a profession subject to all kinds of pressures, criticisms, and calls for change, secure as I can be at my stage of the game that besides being responsible for the education of students in my classroom, I have a responsibility to gain a voice in whatever decisions are made that affect the school as a social-educational organization? I will consider this book successful in its purposes if it helps you to see what you can do for yourself in making a career choice. Aside from reading a book like this and talking with others who you think may be helpful, you cannot avoid looking into, assessing, questioning who and what you are. In that respect, you are the expert, although bear in mind that experts seek second opinions (sometimes!).

This book does not contain all you need to know in making a career choice. It would be more correct to say that you are not in the position of being able to absorb all you "need" to know. I have restricted myself to those issues that have not received the emphasis my experience has led me to conclude they deserve. I have deliberately avoided giving you facts, discussing studies, using jargon, or going on at great length. The chapters are short, I hope their central themes are clear, and I would be gratified no end if what follows caused you to think and willingly to seek to gain more knowledge about a career in teaching, a career of supreme importance at a time when the general public and many in the educational community are bewitched, bothered, and bewildered about how our schools can be improved.

WHO IS "YOU"?

*i*t was and still is the case that a large majority of those who contemplate a career in teaching are women. The reasons are several. First, women are still regarded as the primary caretakers of children. That view is changing, I know, but slowly. In our society, women are seen as uniquely prepared to rear and understand young children; that is, more than men, they, by virtue of biology, role, and experience, "know" children. That is why in our elementary schools, the number of men teachers is truly minuscule. How many men have you seen as teachers in nursery schools and kindergartens? From observations over a long lifetime, *my* answer is *none*. Indeed, it is probably the case that if a man seeks to become a kindergarten teacher, his motivations and personal stability will be suspect.

This state of affairs changes, but not all that dramatically, when we look at our middle and high schools, where there is more than a sprinkling of men. Here again, the explanation reflects attitudes very much a part of our culture: as children grow older, they "need" a firm hand, which, of course, men are "supposed" to have. As children enter and experience the turmoil of adolescence, the male who seeks to teach them, far from being viewed as suspect, is seen as an appropriate role model. The child who leaves elementary school no longer requires the degree of caring and compassion of a mother substitute but rather the firm, authoritative, directive features of a man. That is why until relatively recently most middle and high school principals—as well as superintendents of schools and other administrators— were men. And, let us remember, up until the rise of militant teacher unions, high school teachers had higher salaries, a fact that also seemed right, natural, and proper.

If this state of affairs is changing, it is not because these changes were initiated and welcomed by those who administer our schools but because of changing societal attitudes due to a number of factors, not the least of which was the women's liberation movement. But there was one other factor: beginning in the sixties—a time when every major institution in our country was under critical attack from diverse groups—an increasing number of young men saw a career in teaching as a way of contributing to much needed reforms in our society. Men became more numerous in our schools, but primarily in middle and high schools.*

These changes, however, in no way contradict the fact that when men and women contemplate a career in education, it tends to be from very different perspectives and expectations. What would be surprising would be if that were not the case.

* I wish to emphasize that whatever I have said about men and women in education—their numbers, psychological differences, and assigned social roles—should be understood in terms of *American* society. There are other societies in which the picture is *very* different; where, for example, men predominate in teaching, even in elementary schools. It is parochial in the extreme to assume that the way we see men and women in education has the status of immutable, revealed knowledge.

Being a man or woman is a difference that makes a difference in *any* society, and that includes ours. You may resent, resist, or accept these consequences, but it is in your self-interest to seek to understand why those consequences arose and how you might think about and cope with them. That is the purpose of this book: to consider the different factors that have to be taken into account in contemplating a career in education. That is as true for a career in medicine, law, social work, business, or architecture as it is for education. Every field of endeavor has its pluses and minuses. Every field—including those that are conventionally considered the most "prestigious"—contains more than a few people who, for one or another reason, are dissatisfied with their career. It is very hard for people to say out loud that they are dissatisfied with their vocational choice. It is even hard for some to say it to themselves, except now and then when intruding thoughts flash through their heads in the quiet of their nights.

If men and women contemplate career choice in education from different perspectives, neither of the two groups is homogeneous in this regard. For example, although I assume that most women desire marriage in their future, the mix of marriage and teaching may be perceived quite differently. Some women will plan that if and when they start a family, they will stop working for a period of time—it may be for one or several years—and then return to teaching. Other women will have no intention to stop working except for a period of weeks or a few months. And there are women who have no intention of having a family and for whom teaching will be an uninterrupted career. There is still another subgroup of women (as there are men) who never contemplated a teaching career but at a later point in their lives, and for diverse reasons, seriously consider such a career. It may be because becoming a teacher is, for practical reasons, the career most accessible to them or that they are dissatisfied with whatever job they have and see a career in teaching as more challenging, fulfilling, or secure.

In the case of men, there are those who see teaching as entrance to a profession in which men are in short supply, it has a perceived degree of financial security, there is a degree of autonomy not to be underestimated, and, if it is a profession not accorded the degree of respect it deserves, it is still a socially respected profession, an important one that requires neither defense or explanation. Some of these men undoubtedly would have preferred, *all things being equal,* to enter a more prestigious, higher income profession. But all things are rarely equal! For reasons of economics, family background, and race and ethnicity, teaching holds out more than a few rewards over a lifetime. I must point out that at a place like Yale, the number of men (or women) who enter its tiny teacher preparation program is indeed minuscule. And if the numbers are very, very small, the number of men is not far above zero. Only in the turbulent sixties were the numbers somewhat higher. If those were days of social crusades, it is still the case today that among men who contemplate a teaching career, the social worth of teaching is in the picture.

In my experience, among men more than among women, teaching is seen as a first step in a career ladder at the top of which are a variety of administrative positions. That difference is growing less noticeable. There are men who, initially at least, do not think in terms of moving "up and out of" teaching. For some men their thinking does not change with the passing years. But many more do not start at the bottom of the ladder in order to stay there. They seek elevated positions, more income, more authority. Granted, the "societal atmosphere" is changing and will continue to change. But that is no warrant to gloss over or deny that in our society, men and women have different perspectives about careers, whether in education or elsewhere.

This is not a book about psychology, sociology, or social history. It is about a particular career choice: teaching. What I have endeavored to do in these introductory remarks is to indicate that the "you" in the title of this book refers to a variety of subgroups, each of which contemplates the choice in somewhat different ways.

If these remarks explain the title of the book, they do not explain why I have written this book. So bear with me while I relate my experience, observations, and studies of college seniors contemplating a choice of career, primarily in medicine or law. For those readers interested in a full account, I would suggest they peruse my book *Work, Aging, and Social Change.** The title was a most unfortunate one, because it does not convey the fact that the book is about *young* people in the process of making a career choice, a choice about which they had little uncertainty but that reflected a dramatic ignorance of the lifetime implications of that choice. I shall restrict myself to those choosing medicine as a career, and to a few of our findings.

The stimulus for our studies was the observation that truly sea-swell changes were taking place in medicine, changes that many older physicians were viewing with anger, fear, and regret. The long and short of it was that they resented the increasing loss of professional freedom and authority, the mountains of paperwork third-party payers required, the escalating number of malpractice suits, and a perceived lowering in the esteem of the

* Sarason, S. B. *Work, Aging, and Social Change.* New York: Free Press, 1977.

profession. Many of them no longer saw hospitals as hospitable but rather places administered by nonphysicians unknowledgeable about or insensitive to practitioners. As more than a few of these physicians (ranging in age from forty-five to seventy) said, "I would not like to see my children choose medicine as a career." It is not crucial or even relevant to judge or evaluate the conclusions of these physicians. The important point is that in midcareer or beyond, these physicians felt as they did. This is *not* to say that they no longer experienced personal rewards from their work but rather that the balance between pluses and minuses was far from what they had anticipated. I should also point out that what they related to me was in interpersonal contexts that, if not legally confidential, permitted them to be very frank. What they said was not in answer to a formal survey or interview. I was seen, I think validly, as an interested, sympathetic ear; that is, someone who was trying to understand how the world was changing. In any event, these informal discussions led me to conclude that these physicians were not wildly unrepresentative of their age cohorts.

So we decided to interview (this was in the seventies) college seniors contemplating a career in medicine. Here are a few of our findings:

1. A fair number of seniors resented having to make a choice at that particular time—not because they were so uncertain about the choice but rather because they wanted the opportunity to experience more of this world before "settling down." In some inchoate way, they intuited that once they started medical education, they were "locked in." Whereas previous generations were eager to be locked in, these seniors felt otherwise.

2. When asked why they chose medicine, a large number of them replied that medical education and practice contained a diversity of fields that would prevent narrowness of outlook and experience. In medicine, they said, you had many options. What these students apparently did not know was that not too long after entering medical school, they would be subject to strong pressures to choose *a* specialty, and once they chose a specialty, they would have to make long-term decisions, each of which had the effect of "locking" them in.

3. The students were asked: "What satisfaction do you expect from a career in medicine?" The most frequent answer was that they would have the financial means to travel. What they apparently did not know is that travel, other than for short periods of time, would be difficult for economic and competitive reasons, as well as for fulfilling obligations to sick people. What was most strange is that not a single individual said that they chose medicine for satisfaction of the desire to help people. It could be that that kind of satisfaction was taken for granted. But that does not quite explain why it was *never* mentioned. If the absence or weak strength of that motivation represents a change from what students in earlier decades said, it clearly has implications for how today's students will experience their careers *and* how the general public will come to see and experience them. The motivations powering career choice have life-long consequences.

These findings (and others) led me to a conclusion as important as it is obvious: career choice requires, if only for reasons of self-interest, as much concrete knowledge about "life" in that profession and about one's motivations and expectations as one can gain. At the point where one is making a decision, there is the understandable tendency to be far more aware of the pluses than of the minuses; that is, to make the process of decision making less conflictful, less complex. And too frequently we avoid seeking knowledge and self-understanding because we unreflectively assume that we know what we should know. In no way am I suggesting that it is possible to know as much as one "needs" to know, that it is possible not only to take all relevant factors into account but to weigh each of them appropriately. That is not in the human cards! Nevertheless, if we are imperfect organisms, let us face that fact and try to do the best we can. Choosing a career is like choosing a mate: it is fateful (in the short and long term) and too fraught with diverse considerations to be made lightly. We are used to hearing that in choosing a mate, love is not enough. Similarly, the fact that you are enamored of becoming a certain kind of professional is a necessary but not sufficient reason for choosing to enter that profession. So, if becoming a teacher very much appeals to you, you meet *one* of the criteria on the basis of which you should make a final decision.

Neither I nor anyone else needed to do studies to make the point that *all* professions have undergone dramatic changes in the post–World War II era. One way of characterizing that era is to say that it is one during which there has been a redefinition—on the part of both the general public and those in the professions—of what those professions are or should be. The scope and depth of redefinition have varied among the professions, but *none* has been exempt. To name only a few, nursing, clinical psychology, social work, medicine, and education have experienced the redefinition process to a discernible, even dramatic degree. The outlook and expectations of those in these professions are not the outlook and expectations of those of earlier decades. Hospitals have changed, clinics and social agencies have changed, and schools have changed. It would be more correct to say that these sites have changed as reactions to changes in the larger society. And it is no less correct to say that they are continuing to change. And it should occasion no surprise when I say that these changes have been experienced by people in these professions with mixed feelings, ranging from dismay to enthusiasm.

It is not happenstance that education occupies such a prominent place in the national psyche. It has always occupied an important place, but in a cyclical fashion; that is, every ten years or so, there would be a "great debate" about the inadequacies of our schools, recommendations for reform would be proclaimed and made, and that was that until, several years later, similar and new issues would erupt into national consciousness. That is no longer the case. Concerns about our schools are persistent, become sources of controversies, and increasingly translate into radical calls for change. If this is not known to anyone contemplating a career in education, that person has no business entering the profession! And I say that as much to protect such individuals from personal disaster as to protect the interests of the larger society.

Is the bottle half-empty or half-full? If you perceive it as half-empty, you would not be likely warmly to support an individual's decision to become a teacher. You are likely to ask that individual to consider alternative professions not under such pressure to change, not subject to as much criticism, not as likely to be as so interpersonally demanding and taxing.

If you perceive the bottle as half-full, you would likely say to the individual that he or she is entering teaching at the right, most exciting time: schools are changing, traditions are being questioned, roles are expanding, new challenges are guaranteed, life will never be dull, and schools will continue to be unexcelled places in which to observe social change.

It is obvious that I would not have written this book if I had not been convinced that a career in education can be rewarding over a lifetime; that is, *for some people, whose numbers are not few.* And, as I have suggested, "rewarding" does not mean that such a career traverses a smooth, well-paved, pothole-free road guaranteeing a state of continuous "happiness." By "rewarding" I mean that such a career exposes you to personal and professional challenges, broadens your understanding of self and your society, and holds out the opportunity to improve the education of children and to play a role in altering our schools so as to make that improvement more likely. Teaching takes place in encapsulated classrooms in encapsulated schools, but despite such encapsulation, classrooms and schools reflect every major asset and deficit in our society. If our schools are far from the level of effectiveness we need and desire, it stems in part (and only in part) from our failure to recognize that *unless the conditions for productive learning and development exist for teachers, they, the teachers, cannot create and long sustain those conditions for students.* That places a special challenging obligation on teachers to seek to alter our schools to make those conditions possible.

I am here making a point of crucial significance to anyone contemplating a career in teaching, because it requires that you give up the conventional imagery of an isolated teacher in an isolated classroom. A teacher is part of a very complicated social-professional organization called a school, which in turn is embedded in a complicated scheme called a school system. By virtue of that embeddedness, that teacher is mightily influenced by the structure, character, and traditions of that organization. Not only must the teacher comprehend that embeddedness, but he or she must feel a responsibility to seek a role in governing and altering that organization, which is so fateful for all those within it. Teaching is not or should not be for those unwilling or unable to be active agents of educational-institutional change. From the standpoint of the larger society, there is too much at stake to allow teachers to be passive participants in the dynamics and processes of change. If the larger society has yet to give adequate recognition to that point, it is due to several factors, not the least of which is that those who seek to become teachers have been woefully unprepared to understand and deal with the realities of the culture of our schools.

This book is based on the premise that the more you know about what life in a school entails, the better able you will be to cope actively with the inevitably thorny personal and professional problems that arise. That is no more or less true for the person seeking a corporate career, or one in medicine, architecture, law, government, or the church. Career choice should be powered by ideals. But it is well if it is accompanied by the knowledge that, so to speak, there is no free lunch; that is, you will always be paying a price, there will always be minuses. What one seeks to avoid is becoming a person who knows the price of everything and the value of nothing.

I do not in this book attempt to persuade or dissuade a reader about a career in education. No reader needs to be told that teachers perform an absolutely crucial, fateful role. And no one needs to be told that we are living in times when we are agonizingly aware that schools are far from what we wish them to be. And, I shall assume, no one needs to be told that what happens to present and future efforts at reform will in part be determined by the changing character of those who will be entering the profession. The implication, of course, is that unless there is a change in who seeks to enter the profession, the fruits of the reform efforts will lack sweetness. And this book asserts that we have an obligation to those contemplating a career in teaching to inform and sensitize them to the realities they will encounter.

In the next chapter, I shall take up issues surrounding the question, *When* does an individual contemplate a career in teaching? As we shall see, that seemingly easy-to-answer question is embroiled in controversy about *the knowledge and experience* a person should have *before* entering a preparatory program.

chapter 3

WHEN SHOULD
YOU DECIDE?

*M*ost people currently teach-
ing, or, for that matter, in administrative positions, seriously
considered entering the profession within their first two years of
college. A fair number, mostly women, had already made the
decision when they became undergraduates. Indeed, up until
World War II, a large majority of those entering the profession
enrolled in a state college for teachers, testimony to the fact that
the decision had been made during high school years. After
World War II, those very specialized colleges, some of which
were two-year programs, became or were absorbed into four-
year liberal arts colleges. That came about primarily because of
the dramatic increase in the number of people—mostly veterans
eligible under the generous GI Bill of Rights—seeking a liberal
arts education. It came about primarily for economic reasons
and not because of any articulated dissatisfaction with what
teachers' colleges had been doing, although there had always
been individuals critical of these preparatory programs.

If that absorption was in any way intended to change and
improve the preparation of educators, those intentions ran
headlong into one of the most socially impactful consequences

of World War II: the so-called baby boom. As the dimensions of that boom became clear, it was obvious that there would be, as there was, a shortage of teachers. As a result, many states relaxed their requirements about who could teach in the classroom. It became possible for a college graduate possessing no credentials for teaching to assume such a role in September after taking one or two education courses in the previous summer and agreeing to pursue full credentials while teaching. I personally knew of situations that were so desperate at the opening of the school year that a school system allowed individuals without summer preparation to take over a classroom. As one superintendent said to me, "If the person has one head, a warm body, and a B.A., I can employ them."

Three factors contributed to the teacher shortage. The first is that with the disappearance of teachers' colleges, there was a tendency for the decision to enter teaching to be made somewhat later than in earlier times. The second was that in order to fulfill requirements of a liberal arts curriculum, the decision to enter teaching could, had to, be postponed, usually to the end of the second undergraduate year. There was a third factor that became fateful for the field as the years went on: as the education and liberal arts programs became part of the same institution, questions began to be raised about when an individual should make the career decision—not only when the decision should be made but whether it should be made at all. The controversial question was: should anyone be permitted to enter a preparatory program during the undergraduate years? It was not lost on those who answered in the negative that the shortage of teachers was permitting noncredentialed college graduates to become teachers. Were these people as adequate as, more adequate than, or less adequate than teachers who had completed an undergraduate preparatory program? We shall return to this question—which continues to be very much with us today—in a moment. Let me make the final point that for some people, what is happening in the society at large very much determines when they make a career choice to enter teaching. I refer specifically to those who never contemplated such a career until the opportunity quickly to do so arose. The fact is that then (as now) there were many people who would seriously contemplate a career in education if it did not require a year or two of full-time schooling with undue financial sacrifice. There are reasons to believe that their numbers are greater today than immediately after World War II, especially as it is the case today that many college graduates are unemployed or fear losing their jobs. The general point is that what happens in the society at large is not unrelated to when a career choice is made and, even more significant, to how experiencing that career over the years will vary.

Let us return to the controversial question that really got articulation and force in the turbulent sixties, when every major institution in our society was, it is fair to say, under attack. Public dissatisfaction with our schools, especially in urban areas, was loud and clear. Schools were inadequate, they had to change or be changed, and a new breed of teachers had to replace those whose education, training, and outlook were counter-productive. There were several parts to the argument that entering teaching should be postponed to the postcollege years. The first part was that undergraduate preparatory programs left insufficient time to allow students to be steeped in the subject matters they would teach. How could teachers with a superficial comprehension of subject matter convey that subject matter to students? The second part was that four years of a liberal arts education was an acceptable minimum for enlarging and deepening a person's knowledge and intellectual horizons. That is to say, such an education is a way of comprehending humanity's achievements and problems now and in the near and distant past. A "liberal" education is one that liberates you from the negative consequences of narrowness, prejudice, and unreflectively assimilated myths. There was a third part to the argument, which tended not to be articulated clearly, and it concerned age and experience; that is, teaching is too important a societal function to be carried out by people who have not "lived," whose experience in and of this world is limited. If a full liberal arts education was by no means a guarantee of personal and intellectual maturity, it was a minimally acceptable criterion, far better than a watered-down one.

This controversy had one clear result: in colleges having teacher preparation programs, the number of their requirements was reduced and the liberal arts requirements were increased. This has not satisfied those who regard preparation for a career in education as desirable only at the graduate level.

It was during the sixties that many school systems scoured the country in order to attract graduates of liberal arts colleges—especially those regarded as "prestigious," if not elitist—to teaching. As before, segments of the educational community were far from enthusiastic about placing untrained individuals in the classroom. And again, as before, the controversial question never received study. I and my colleagues had a good deal of experience with these recruits. We were forced to the conclusion that their unfamiliarity with classrooms and schools made for a very trying and upsetting baptism into a teaching career. But it was also true that fully credentialed beginning teachers did not have an easy time of it. As a group, beginning teachers, credentialed or not, were in agreement that there was much they had not known about teaching and schools *that they could or should have known;* that is, how one experienced teaching was less a matter of when one began teaching than it was of sheer knowledge of what life was like in classrooms, schools, and school systems. That, I must add, is what one hears from physicians starting a practice and lawyers in their first position. It is, in my opinion, a valid generalization that anyone contemplating a professional career cannot assume that their preparation for that career will provide them other than an "acceptable minimum" in regard to the personal, organizational, and professional problems that they will inevitably encounter. This book is an effort to indicate that people contemplating a career in education have to assume some responsibility to raise and pursue questions that will give them a more realistic and rounded picture of the practical implications of their choice.

Beginning in the late eighties, another "movement" to attract and place new liberal arts graduates in schools, primarily inner-city ones, was started. In fact, it was spearheaded by a Princeton University graduate, and it received a good deal of publicity as well as corporate and foundation support. From both newspaper accounts and personal knowledge (obtained serendipitously), I know that a fair number of these recruits dropped out after their first year of experience. The reasons, I am sure, are many, but certainly one of them is that they were unprepared for teaching real children in real schools where problems abound.

All of the above is prologue to this question: on what basis should a person contemplating a career in teaching decide whether to seek credentials in the undergraduate years or to postpone that seeking to postgraduate years? For some people, the decision will be made on very practical grounds; that is, economics and geography. For others, it will be made on grounds of uncertainty about an early choice and/or a need for a longer period of time during which alternative choices can be explored or simply the desire to get as broad an education as possible. Let us begin with this latter heterogeneous group, if only because it raises a most fundamental point about how a near term decision should be embedded in one's picture of development over a lifetime.

At least in the abstract, readers will agree that one should not seek a college education merely to get a diploma. A college education has three purposes. The first is to gain an understanding of the world we live in, not only an *American* world but also the world beyond our borders, a world increasingly interconnected in myriad ways. The second is to understand how the modern world came about; that is, the role of religion, science, technology, social forces, the arts, and what, for the sake of brevity, I shall call ideas and philosophies. The third purpose is that the first two purposes should serve to help the student ponder how and where one wants to be in this world; that is, how one wants to live one's life and why.

That is a very tall order, the success of which depends not only on the quality of faculty and the scope of course offerings but also on the personal-intellectual motivation of the student. One should not go to college with the stance that you are an empty vessel waiting to be filled with facts. Granted, one expects the faculty to present material in an organized and interesting way—not only organized but a stimulus to the questions and interests of the student. Nevertheless, one also expects that the student is motivated to play an active role, to be a seeker, an organizer, a questioner.

Am I describing the ideal situation? Yes and no. Yes in the

sense that too many college courses do not meet their intended purposes and too many students do not actively utilize and capitalize on their interests, questions, and abilities. No in the sense that to regard it as ideal is to overlook one of its most practical consequences or implications: over the course of your adult years, the need and desire to comprehend your world, far from decreasing or remaining constant, increases. Concomitantly, the need to feel that one makes a difference in this world also increases.

Why is it that we regard failure to be graduated from high school to be personally and socially self-defeating? The question can be answered in several ways, but one of them is fateful: as the years go on, these individuals find themselves keenly regretting not only their limited knowledge of their world but, no less important, that plaguing feeling that they will never feel a sense of personal growth, that sense without which living is a very humdrum affair. "If I knew then what I know now . . ." We have all said that about one or another aspect of our lives, but when we say that about "lost opportunities" our daily lives never let us forget, it is hard to take.

I am *not* saying that the more formal education you have, the better off you will be as a person. What I am saying is that if you are the kind of person who actively *seeks* education as a way of understanding yourself and your world, you increase your chances that you will experience that sense of growth. Regardless of choice of career, education should not be viewed only as a way of acquiring knowledge and technical skills but as a way of exploring and expanding your understanding of yourself in relation to humanity's history, accomplishments, and purposes. That is an obligation you owe to yourself for the very practical reason that such exploration and expansion will help you avoid the passive stance to forging your future. Acquiring an education does not make you an educated person. An educated person is one who *seeks* to understand what this world has been and is and how that explains, if only in part, what that person is and wants to become.

I have italicized *seek* for two reasons. The first is general: anyone contemplating a choice of career should take responsibility for the scope and direction of their education, not unreflectively fit into a mold predetermined by others. There is too much at stake over the lifetime to allow one's education to be largely determined by others. You are a unique individual in terms of your background, patterns of interest, curiosities, and questions. To ignore that uniqueness is to ignore what has given meaning to your life, to push underground what has powered your outlook and perspective.

The second reason is peculiar to those contemplating a teaching career: to teach children requires—I would say demands—that you never forget that children are seeking, questing, exploring, curious organisms trying to make sense of themselves and their worlds. The teacher is not someone whose only task is to convey facts and knowledge and to help children acquire a variety of procedural skills. That is an important task, but no less important is how to discharge that task taking account of the seekings of children; that is, how to meld the world of children with the world of adults. *Whatever I have said about the seekings of those contemplating a teaching career is no less applicable to children in the classroom.* If our schools are far from what we would like them to be, it is in part because we are far more aware of what *we* want children to learn than we are of what *they* want to learn; that is, the whys and wherefores that occupy their worlds. Contemplating a career in teaching requires that you know what such a professional preparation entails, what others have concluded you need to learn. Without in any way suggesting that such a preparation is without merit or to be taken lightly, the fact remains that you should not fall into the trap of assuming that that preparation takes into account your diverse interests, needs, and seekings. In fact, as I shall discuss in later chapters, that preparation too often assumes a degree of ignorance on your part that is wholly unjustified; that is, you know far more, you have experienced far more than the formal, predetermined program acknowledges.

It is obvious that in the abstract I recommend that a career in teaching should be postponed until the graduate years. I must reiterate that I do not make that recommendation because there is secure evidence that those who gain their preparation during their undergraduate years are, *by conventional criteria*, not as good teachers as those who gained it after the undergraduate years. The recommendation is made on the basis of the belief that the more you take advantage of the opportunity to sample and explore what can be called, for the sake of brevity, the arenas of human history, accomplishments, and problems, the more likely you are to experience and reinforce the importance of seeking and the sense of personal-intellectual growth. The logo of my travel agent was "See the world before you leave it." The logo that encapsulates what I have tried to say is "Seek the world before you leave it." My late and lamented travel agent had two characteristics of the good teacher. He *never* put us up in places he had not visited, and he strove valiantly and successfully (in our case) to take account of a client's needs, interests, seekings. He taught us, and we taught him.

If a person is able to postpone entering a preparatory program until after college, it does not mean that he or she should not actively seek to gain experience in or around schools. What those experiences might be, their diversity and duration, and who can facilitate contacts with schools depend on numerous factors, not the least of which is the (again) seeking and persistence of the individual. If my experience is any guide, even in colleges that have no departments of education, there is always at least one faculty member who has an interest, research or otherwise, in schools. Many colleges have a center for volunteer activity. And, let us not forget, one can ask for an appointment with a local superintendent of schools, or with a principal, to seek advice and help about volunteering one's time in mutually rewarding ways. The point is that by using one's own initiative, one can gain experience relevant to a career in teaching. Informal experience can be very valuable. But the student has to have the attitude that the more he or she has school-relevant experiences, the more secure the individual will feel about a career choice. Whatever the benefits of formal courses, they are not the only ways your horizons can be broadened and deepened. Taking responsibility for one's own education should not be confused with taking courses.

Now for the realities of economics and geography, realities many individuals face. I am referring to those whose economic resources are so limited, in whom the pressures to be gainfully employed are such, as to make it impossible to postpone career choice until after the college years. They have to enroll in a college that has an undergraduate teacher preparatory program, and that usually means a nearby state college. In the past and in the present, these undergraduate programs prepare by far a majority of those in teaching. It is one thing in the abstract to recommend that these undergraduate programs should be phased out or eliminated. It is quite another thing to fail to recognize that many who seek a career in teaching cannot afford to extend their formal education. We are here dealing with a public policy question that has not received the attention it deserves. In the abstract, I have no quarrel with those who recommend eliminating undergraduate preparatory programs. In the "real world," however, the practical implications of such a proposal have to be faced. Who teaches in our schools has always been determined by the factors of economics and gender. To gloss over this fact is to bury one's head in the sands of fantasy.

As I indicated earlier, over the years the amount of time an undergraduate preparatory program can require of students has decreased. To the critics of these programs, that is a desirable state of affairs. To the faculty of these programs, that state of affairs unduly waters down professional preparation. One consequence has been that in many states, teachers are required to take education-relevant courses after they have begun teaching. There is a difference between *wanting* to take courses and being *required* to do so, and in saying that, we are back to the role of *seeking*; that is, to the perception that it is in one's self-interests to gain as much knowledge and understanding as one's circumstances permit. Seeking cannot be legislated. It can be engendered and reinforced in countless ways in the course of one's educational experiences. Is it not the case that there are teachers, whether prepared at the undergraduate or graduate level, who would very much like to pursue their special interests that may not be *directly* relevant to their professional activities? Should not such a pursuit be encouraged, facilitated, and rewarded no less than when they take mandated postgraduate courses?

I think I have said enough to persuade the reader that *when* one contemplates entering teaching raises thorny issues for both the individual and the field of education. They are not new issues. If in recent decades they have taken on a greater saliency, it is because of a general public concern with the inadequacies of our schools. What the reader contemplating a career in teaching probably does not know is that *these issues are not peculiar to a career in teaching in particular and education in general. They are complex, controversy-arousing issues in the preparation of physicians, lawyers, psychologists, social workers, and others. Whenever and wherever one deals with professional education, the timing and balance between general and professional education become issues, and one encounters differences of opinion, polarizations, and heated argument.* What would be truly surprising would be if that were not the case. Education is not a special case. The grass is not greener elsewhere.

Take the following "assertions" about the selection and preparation of physicians, assertions, I can assure the reader, that are embedded in heated debate.

1. Requiring an individual to choose a medical career in the undergraduate years dramatically skews his or her education in the direction of the sciences at the expense of a broad liberal arts exposure.
2. That skewing drastically limits his or her understanding of the world he or she lives in and the changing place and perception of medicine by that "external" world. (Just as the general public views educators as living in a "world of their own," so do they view physicians, and these views are not all that favorable.)
3. Too many physicians lack that degree of caring and compassion necessary to comprehend the plight of sick people. (Just as in education there is the maxim that *we teach children, not subject matter,* in medicine the maxim is that

you treat people, not their bodies. In both fields, the maxims are too often honored in the breach, not in practice.)

4. The professional preparation of physicians does not adequately prepare them for the realities of independent practice and how that practice may or will change them as people.

For these and other assertions, the debate is long-standing, raging, and important. The point here is not where you stand in relation to such assertions but the brute fact that these issues are real issues in all of the major professions.

What does this mean for someone contemplating a career in teaching? It requires that you very deliberately assume the responsibility to seek (again seek!) as much knowledge as you can about the implications of different decisions you will have to make. If you cannot be expected to gain all of the knowledge you need, that is no excuse for passivity. After all, contemplating such a decision is not like deciding whether you should dine in restaurant A or B. Even in the case of choosing a restaurant, especially if it is for a special occasion, you do not choose at random. You feel more secure the more information you already have or can get from others. Contemplating a career in teaching is more akin to contemplating a trip to a foreign country: you can read about that country, talk to people who have been there, determine costs, language barriers, and tourist traps, and begin to get up a priority list reflective of your *interests and available time.* The more active the seeking the more likely the trip will be rewarding, and the less likely that on returning home you will regret having taken the trip.

chapter 4

WHY TEACHING?

*t*here is always more than one reason why we choose a particular career. If that is a glimpse of the obvious, it is also true that we tend not to pursue the implications of the different propelling factors. So, for example, if an individual chooses a career in banking, it is very likely that a major reason is the expectation of earning increasing amounts of income over time, amounts that by conventional standards are far above average. But such an individual is not likely to say publicly that a high income is the only reason determining choice. Desiring a high income is associated with imagery about life-style; that is, the kind of home one envisions, the material possessions that in part define for that person "the good life," the types of social organizations with which he or she wishes to affiliate, the kinds of schools he or she wants his or her children to experience, the sense of security that one is in a career relatively immune to the yo-yo features of the economy, and more. Nor is that individual likely to say out loud that being in a position of *power*—making decisions that mightily can affect the lives of others—is important in his or her makeup. What the individual will say is that a banker is in a respected, important position enabling him or her to be helpful to the plans of others. Although all these bankers-to-be will say that such a career is an interesting one in which one can observe and learn a great deal about people, the community, and the world generally, there will be wide individual differences in the weight they place on and the clarity with which they perceive the factor of "interest."

The point here is that there are public and private reasons entering into a choice of career. What we say publicly is what we think is socially acceptable. *Some* of what we keep private reflects the perception that these motives may be misunderstood or criticized. And it is also the case that some of what we keep private we may ourselves view with suspicion. I am being descriptive, not judgmental. My remarks are for the purpose of emphasizing that in choosing a career, one must come to grips with the different motivations that are propelling you to consider a particular career. Yes, you have to try to "know thyself" in order to ask and answer a crucial and practical question: What is the likelihood that your different motivations will find satisfactory expression in the contemplated career? It is wildly unrealistic to expect that at the point of career choice a young person—or an older one considering switching into teaching—can answer the question in detail or depth. But that is no excuse for avoiding the question and not seeking as comprehensive an answer as possible. The fact of life is that even after you have made a choice, and even after you have entered the profession, that question will arise again and again. To the extent that you tried to confront and answer that question, you will be better able to judge whether you wish to remain in that profession or in that particular part of it. The same question can be (will be) answered in different ways, depending on experiences.

Let me tell you about two kinds of students I came to know

during my forty-five years as a teacher in a doctoral program for psychologists. Suffice it to say this graduate program selected students who expressly stated that they sought a research career in psychology. Indeed, if in their application for admission they said little or nothing about a research career, those applicants were rejected even if all "objective" evidence (like test scores or grades) was very high. If a student was admitted, the assumption was that there was a meeting of minds about motivation for a research career.

The first group of students were those who after the first or second year of graduate work came to the conclusion that a career in psychological research either was not for them or had to be put much lower on their priority list. What they came to conclude was that teaching psychology would be far more interesting and stimulating than doing research. They wanted to be a certain kind of psychologist. In no way did they want to leave the field. At the same time, they took satisfaction in "finally" knowing what they wanted their career to be. They also felt some guilt that they would not fulfill the professional objectives of the program. One can ask: could these students have known before entering the graduate program that research was an iffy career for them? Maybe yes, maybe no. The important point is that they had the courage to learn from their experience that a research career was not for them.

The second group were graduate students who for several or more years had been fully credentialed public school teachers. They now sought a research career in psychology. In no instance did they regard their experience in schools as wasteful, unimportant, uninteresting, or uninstructive. Far from it, they wanted to capitalize on their classroom experiences by broadening their knowledge and horizons. Teaching had been fulfilling up until they became aware that the questions and problems their experiences engendered required a change in career.

What "lessons" may be drawn from these two groups (which can be found in any profession)? There is, in my opinion, one major conclusion: choosing a career is a starting point in a *developmental* process the course of which is far from predictable. That is not to say it is unpredictable but rather that one should expect that experience will in some way alter how you perceive and weigh the different factors contributing to your choice of career. There is a second conclusion: it is in your self-interest continuously to judge the degree to which your choice of career is changing, if it is, or meeting your personal needs, interests, and motivations. And there is a third conclusion: the more and the earlier you keep these issues in the forefront of your mind, the more likely you will seek and consider practical options more likely to meet your needs.

Why do people seek a teaching career in our schools? One of the more frequent reasons is that they like children and they would enjoy a role in which they would influence their development. Put another way, teaching is challenging, interesting, and mutually interpersonally rewarding. This reason is reflected in the conventional imagery of a teacher in a classroom: an adult instructing, guiding, supervising, and motivating children. The responsibility of the teacher is as awesome as it is obvious.

But there is something missing in this frequently given reason, a something potentially knowable but rarely articulated: a classroom contains an assortment of young characters who vary, sometimes wildly, in motivation, conduct, likability, and style of learning. The conventional image of the teacher is of someone who not only likes all children in his or her classroom but is capable of being equally effective with each of them. That, of course, is nonsense. There are many parents who in their heart of hearts know that they do not like each of their children to the same degree and they are not equally effective with each of them. But many parents expect of teachers what they expect but find they cannot experience with their own children. Why do I say that this is potentially knowable to someone contemplating a teaching career? Because that person has spent years as a student in classrooms and has observed the obvious: teachers, rhetoric aside, are like everyone else in that they cannot like or be equally effective with each child in the classroom. There is one other obvious point personally experienced by that individual: he or she did not like all teachers to the same degree.

The reader would be quite wrong to conclude that I am calling into question the importance or validity or relevance of liking to work with children. The point I am making can be put in a general and specific way. The general way is that in *all* professions requiring you to deal with individuals or groups, it is a fact of life that you will find yourself feeling perplexed and guilty that you do not find all people likable or responsive to your efforts to be helpful. (That, I should hasten to add, does not mean that you are "right" and they are "wrong." It is not as simple as that!) The specific way is that however much you like or love children in the abstract, you will at times find teaching them to require you to question your degree of "liking." Yes, teaching children is interesting and challenging, far more so than is usually implied by the most frequent reason given for contemplating a teaching career. The challenge in such a career inheres in the fact that it is an intellectually, interpersonally demanding career. It is not a career for those requiring peace, tranquility, and a smooth routine. If that is what you require, avoid any profession that brings you into close, even intimate relationships with people. There are many physicians, lawyers, social workers, and even psychologists and psychiatrists who have learned, often too late, this "lesson." And the situation is not all that different in the corporate world!

Those who give the first reason for contemplating a teaching career rarely confront one very important implication of their imagery of a teacher in a classroom. It concerns issues of authority and power, issues implied by such words as *instructing, guiding, supervising,* and *motivating.* People differ a great deal in how they need, seek, and enjoy a position of power-authority. Some people see teaching as a socially acceptable way of satisfying one's need to "be in charge," to exercise power-authority for the purpose of furthering the development of children. That is not only socially acceptable, it is understandable and commendable. After all, if you have such a need, you should choose a career where that need can be satisfied. The problem with such a need is when its strength is such as to become an end and not a means, when it is primarily self-serving and not other-serving, when it renders one insensitive to the needs of others, when it becomes an obstacle to understanding not only others but oneself as well. None of us likes to see ourselves in this way, but the fact is that some of us are that way.

In light of what I said earlier about the variety of personalities in any classroom, the strength of such a need can have enormous consequences for children *and* teacher. Given such a strong need, it is likely that one will unreflectively see any or slight challenges to one's power-authority as instances not to be glossed over or to be handled other than by exercising one's power-authority. What is more consequential is that you are rendered insensitive to the possibility that your style of teaching may not be effective.

It is no secret that a person approaches his or her first day of teaching as a baptism of fire. Will I be able to "control" the class? Will some of the children defy me in some way? Will someone ask me a question I cannot answer or tell me that what I said is wrong? The questions are many and intimidating. Again I should tell the reader that these fantasies (really nightmares) are not peculiar to the beginning teacher. Over the years, I have supervised scores of graduate students in their therapeutic work with patients. In helping students prepare for their first meeting with their first patient, two things were obvious. The first was the level of anxiety that they would mess things up, which, of course, was understandable and for which what I had to offer was, at best, semihelpful. The second—evident in the supervisory session after that first hour—was that some students had such a need to display to appear to be in charge, to be perceived as the ultimate fount of knowledge and wisdom, that they completely missed what the patient thought and felt.

I do not bring these matters up with the expectation that anything I say here will be very illuminating to those with an unduly strong need to be in a position of power-authority. One hopes that in the course of one's preparation for teaching, these matters will be not only raised but dealt with. One cannot count on that. I have brought these matters up for two reasons. The first is to alert readers to the fact that how you view and experience power-authority will very much influence not only the degree of satisfaction you will experience as a teacher but also your effectiveness as a role model for children. The second reason is more general and ultimately more important for society: the personal characteristics of those who enter teaching are differences that make a difference. Anyone entering teaching should not be indifferent to these professional issues. A professional is, among other things, someone who is concerned with any factor that determines the overall quality of those in that profession.

What about those individuals who are very uncomfortable exercising power-authority, who shrink from any such display? Their number, like the first group, is not small. It is certainly no defect in personality to avoid situations where you should or have to take a stand, where you have to be directive, where challenges to your style have to be handled, where extreme reactions of others call forth from you equally extreme, upsetting reactions. It is no defect unless you find yourself, as teachers frequently do, in a role where the exercise of power-authority is predictable. What I am saying is by no means peculiar to teaching. For example, in the corporate world, there are many instances of people promoted to positions of power-authority that bring to the fore their reluctance or inability or conflicts about power-authority. Similarly, it is by no means infrequent in our schools that a teacher promoted to a principalship, or a principal appointed to a superintendency, comes to be seen as ineffective because of his or her reluctance to exercise power-authority for fear of "alienating" or making others "unhappy" or being seen as "dictatorial." There are parents in whom this reluctance is a characteristic.

Some readers may have concluded from what I have said that I regard children as untamed, teacher-devouring, pain-producing creatures whose main goal in classroom life is to make life difficult for teachers. Nothing could be farther from the truth, which is that most children are predisposed to be "good citizens." But that truth should not obscure the other truth that there are times when a teacher has to exercise power-authority, like it or not. The point is that the frequency of such occurrences depends on a number of factors, not the least of which is how congruent such exercise is with the personality or temperament of the teacher; more specifically, whether the teacher has an *unduly* strong or weak need to exercise power-authority. Anyone contemplating a teaching career should not avoid *trying* to come to grips with the kind of person he or she is. In teaching, as in all human service professions, satisfaction from work is very much a function of the interaction between the requirements of role and one's temperament or personality style. Choosing a career is serious business, too serious to gloss over coming to grips with the kind of person you are. In making a choice, you can amass a mountain of facts, but if those facts are not scrutinized in terms of your personal assets and vulnerabilities, you may be doing yourself a disservice.

It may also be that my use of the term *power-authority* has engendered in some readers the image of the teacher as someone who has all of the rights and privileges of an executive, a legislature, and a judiciary; that is, the "ruler" of all he or she surveys. That is to say, the teacher is all powerful and the students are powerless and that is right, natural, and proper! Unfortunately, that image is too frequently seen in practice, which is why some of our classrooms are joyless affairs for students. Instead of power-authority, I could have described the teacher as a leader, or manager, or executive, or director. The important point is that regardless of the label you prefer or employ, the *responsibility* of the teacher is twofold. The first is to give purpose and overall direction to the goals of learning. The second is to do this in a way that capitalizes on the interests of students, helps them assume increasing responsibility for their learning, and allows them realistically to feel that they have a role in determining how life in the classroom will be lived. Put another way, the goal of the teacher is to increase the sense of internal power-authority of students. That sense can never be felt by students assigned the role of passive recipient or onlooker, by students who dutifully go along with the rules and regulations coming from a single source.

The teacher is like the director of a play. The director has read the script, developed imagery of how the different roles should be acted, the subtle points that will have to be brought out, and the problems that will be encountered. The director *directs*. But that director knows one other thing: each of the actors he or she has chosen—or, sometimes, the actors someone else has chosen—is a unique person whose style and personality he or she will have to take into account, a person to whom he or she will have to make some accommodation, a person who will have his or her own ideas of how his or her particular role should be acted, a person not likely to respond passively to the director's imagery and ideas. In brief, the director has to be sensitive to the needs and ideas of others, to "listen" to them, to "hear" them, to seek a basis for agreement or compromise. Some dramatic productions never reach opening night; some do and close quickly; during rehearsals, actors are replaced, and sometimes the director is replaced. The most frequent cause of these failures is that the director was either too authoritarian or too passive to cope with gargantuan egos.

The teacher, like the director, has power-authority, and what makes both roles so fascinating and crucial is how they exercise it. The difference between teaching as routine and as art is the difference between day and night, between "ruling" and "leading," between "pouring in" and "getting out." If you become a teacher, you will have heard scads of times that a teacher teaches children, *not* subject matter; that is, the task of the teacher is always to take account of "where children are" and how to adapt subject matter to those children, each of whom is different. Knowing subject matter is one thing; how to adapt it to very different kinds of children is another thing.

Why did I begin this chapter with power-authority? For one thing, I wanted to suggest to those contemplating a career in education that they examine their imagery about teachers and determine how realistic that imagery is. Yes, liking children is absolutely of bedrock importance, and so is the desire to observe and contribute to their intellectual and personal development. If those motivations are important, they are not sufficient for making a decision, because in real classrooms with real children those motivations will require of you a bottomless well of vigilance, sensitivity, patience, and understanding not only in regard to children but in regard to yourself. John Dewey, one of our greatest psychologists and educators, once said that a public school teacher should receive the same salary as a college professor. He was not seeking to ingratiate himself with teachers. He said that because he understood that teaching is (or should be) a complex, demanding, trying, even exhausting process experienced daily over many months. And he understood that the satisfactions from the process come not only from observing the growth and development of children but, no less importantly, from the sense of growth and development in the teacher. If at the end of the school year a teacher does not feel that sense, it is very likely that he or she has short-changed the students, at least some of them. Teaching is satisfying because it is challenging and demanding; it requires that you never forget your obligations to children *and* yourself: your values and goals. Teaching is not for everybody. That is true for any profession, but not every profession has been given the responsibility of influencing the lives of children.

The reader would be correct in concluding that I regard teaching as awesomely complex. I realize that someone contemplating such a career can, at best, have a very incomplete understanding of that complexity. My aim here has been to alert the reader to what I think is a fact: your image of a teacher is both very incomplete and in many respects wrong. Far from absolving you of responsibility to seek to learn what you can before you make a decision, it should spur you to check your imagery in whatever ways possible. I shall have more to say about this in a later chapter. Let us now turn to another aspect of your imagery: the specific satisfactions you expect to experience in your interactions with your students. If career choice always derives from more than one motivation, one of the most important has to do with expected satisfactions, with "personal rewards," with those experiences that permit you to say, "Teaching is hard but it has been worth it." As we shall see, how well you understand children determines the kinds and frequency of the satisfactions you can expect from them. What satisfactions can you realistically expect from children? Are you the kind of person who needs (or expects) a lot of "personal give" from students?

I said earlier that there are reasons for choosing a career we prefer to keep private or we tell only to close friends. One such reason is that your summers are your own, there is a long Christmas vacation, two or three times during the school year there is a week's break, there is no school on national (sometimes religious) holidays, and the school day usually is over by midafternoon. For those people who have or expect to have a family, those nonworking periods are important. And that is also the case for those whose economic pressures require them to have another part-time job. There are also people who have diverse needs, interests, or hobbies for whom these nonworking periods are a real boon; that is, opportunities to give concrete expression to different aspects of what they are as people. Why are some individuals contemplating a career in teaching uncomfortable saying loudly and clearly that they look forward to having "time to themselves," more time than people in other professions have? One reason is that they have grown up in a culture where "work" is defined as an activity you engage in every day for at least eight hours (more or less, usually more), on the basis of which you "earn" a vacation of two to four weeks. It is not only a defining characteristic, it is an *expectation* we absorb, and so when we contemplate a career in teaching, we may feel guilty that we will have far more "free" time than other people. And in my experience, at the point when the career choice is made, the lure of such free time can be guilt-producing, as if succumbing to that lure suggests something negative about our motivation. It is also likely that the person has heard members of his or her family or community say, "Teachers have an easy time of it. Look at how large a part of the year they have off." It is not surprising if someone contemplating a career in teaching is reluctant to agree publicly with such an assessment.

I see nothing at all wrong in choosing a profession you feel will satisfy your needs, interests, and desired life-style. But (there is always a but) in the case of teaching, the initial lure will look rather different once one enters the profession. What such a neophyte *and* the general public do not comprehend is how physically and intellectually demanding and wearing teaching can be. And I say "can be" for those who do not permit the obligations of productive teaching to be forgotten as one faces daily the awesome task of managing, stimulating, encouraging, empowering a class of very different young characters each of whom is, so to speak, a law unto him- or herself.

I once recommended, only half-facetiously, that each state have a law requiring parents to take over a classroom twice a year. I said that for two reasons. The first was to indicate how truly ignorant most people are of what good teaching requires physically and intellectually. The second reason was to make the point that educators have done a poor job of disabusing the public of the image of *a* teacher standing in front of a group of children "telling" them what to do and how to do it. Yes, there are teachers for whom that image unfortunately is appropriate. But for the others, that image is egregiously misleading.

It is not infrequent these days to hear people who should know better propose that the school year should be lengthened. If their motivation is understandable and well intentioned, it nevertheless displays a lack of comprehension of what goes *into* good teaching and what it takes *out of* teachers. If teachers have, relatively speaking, a lot of "free time," they *need* it. It is not a luxury, an indulgence, a gift.

Why is it that the public never questions federal regulations limiting the number of hours in the week a commercial airplane pilot can fly? The number of hours is small, but they are hours demanding constant vigilance, precise reactions, and a bodily tension that can be debilitating. The stakes are high, of course, and that is why the federal regulations err on the side of caution. The stakes are high in the classroom, too high to underestimate or to gloss over the complexity of teaching and its consequences for teachers. In saying that, I am again referring to teachers who see their task not as the pouring in of knowledge but as the getting out and building upon the curiosities and interests of students. Those who see their task as a pouring-in one are flying blindly without instruments.

To say that you like children does not mean that you will like teaching. That is a point no one contemplating a career in teaching can afford to ignore. What is unfortunate is that many young people do not consider teaching as a career because it does not appear to them to be a challenging role in which all of their capacities will be tested and expressed. They are captives of the conventional imagery of a teacher in front of a class, imagery as unrevealing and misleading as saying that parents "rear" children, a one-directional relationship in which parents "direct" and children dutifully comply with directions. As many parents will attest, rearing children is a two-way street in which both parties are giving and getting, each teaching the other, each learning about the other, and each deriving satisfaction from being with the other. Teaching, like parenting, can be enormously satisfying. And teaching—like parenting or any role requiring you to interact on a sustained basis with other people— is not free of conflict, misgivings, doubts, and second thoughts. As I shall indicate in the next chapter, satisfactions from teaching and parenting are real, albeit far from constant.

chapter 5

SATISFACTION FROM STUDENTS AND PARENTS

*P*ermit me briefly to be autobiographical. I taught at Yale for forty-four years. *Taught* is a misleading verb, because most of my days were occupied with reading, writing, and research (mostly in schools). Rarely did I approach a classroom without saying to myself, "Wouldn't it be nice if I did not have to teach, if I could devote all my time to research and writing?" Once I was in the classroom, the juices would begin to flow, stimulated by many things, the most crucial of which were the comments and questions of students. In that classroom, I became, so to speak, alive. If I was not by conventional standards a superb teacher, I was far from the worst. In that classroom, I gave my all.

From year to year, cohorts of students can vary a great deal in their "aliveness." There were years when the students appeared passive, uncurious, unmotivated, and no joy to be with. They were exceptions, albeit very trying ones. In most years, it would be no more than ten minutes before an exciting discussion got started *among* the students and I was in the position of a moderator of a debate. Those were the times when at the end of the class I felt I had learned and accomplished something worthwhile. I had earned my keep, although if pressed, neither I nor the students could say precisely what had been "learned." Having an intellectually stimulating "good time" is to some people not a valid criterion by which to judge teacher effectiveness. They want to know what facts and skills were assimilated in that class; that is, facts and skills that can be measured by some presumably objective test. I would be the last to deny that the acquisition of skills and knowledge is important. But I would be among the first to say that the overarching goal of a teacher is to light intellectual fires, to make the world of learning and ideas interesting and *self*-propelling; that is, to engender in students the desire to know more. I do not consider the goal to have been achieved if on a test students can give back to you what you taught them. The goal is achieved if in addition they have developed an *interest* in the subject matter, if it has come to have some personal significance for their lives. My most satisfying teaching experiences have been in classrooms where both students and I found our discussions interesting. I will have more to say about this in later chapters.

Why did I have such ambivalence about teaching? The first reason is that I *never* felt I knew as much as I should. If my students probably saw me as a walking encyclopedia, that is not the way I have ever seen myself. That is not undue modesty on my part. Countless times I would hear myself say something at the same time I was agonizingly aware that what I was saying was only part of the "truth" and that I did not know all I should know about that truth. And it should go without saying that there were times when questions were directed to me that indisputably proved (to me, at least) that my knowledge was limited, sometimes nonexistent. My teaching style is such as to encourage questions from students, the more the better. The downside of that style is that sometimes you will get questions that expose your ignorance. The upside of that style is that student questions were for me the major sources of *my* satisfactions in teaching because those questions were of interest to students and it was that interest I sought to engender and reinforce. Too many of our classrooms—in college, secondary schools, and elementary schools—are uninteresting places because student questions are not encouraged to the degree that they should be.

I do not think that my reaction is idiosyncratic. Very experienced actors have said that before each performance, even in a long-running play, they experience some degree of stage fright. Indeed, they also say that not experiencing some degree of stage fright is a warning that they have succumbed to a routine that dilutes both quality and force of performance. Actors tell us they *know* when they have captured the interest of the audience, when it is responsive. Teaching is performing before and with an audience. Knowing that his or her audience has been "captured" is truly a moving, satisfying experience for a teacher.

A second reason for my "stage fright" (why I would rather be elsewhere) is the fear that I will be unable to come up with ways to make ideas have personal meaning for students. I may be confident that I can clearly state an idea or concept, but what can I do to help students relate that idea to something in their lives and background so that they "own" it, it is embedded in their thinking? *Teaching challenges your creativity.* And in the case of the public school teacher, it is a *daily* challenge. If therein lies the challenge, therein also lie both the satisfactions and the dissatisfactions. Not infrequently did I feel I had not adequately met the challenge, and at those times I soothed my ego by saying that at least I tried to meet the challenge. Candor requires that I say that too frequently teachers develop a style that avoids the challenge. If that is understandable, it is not excusable.

The third reason is wrapped up in the question, What satisfactions keep you going, sustain you, over a career in teaching? In my case, having taught only on the undergraduate and graduate levels, the rewards have been of three kinds. The first, implied in the first two reasons, is your own feeling that you have been meeting your goals consistent with the values on which they are set. Others may judge you otherwise, but in your heart of hearts, you know you did your best, you did not succumb to routine, apathy, resignation. (That is no less a criterion for an elementary school teacher than for a college professor.) A second kind of reward is when students in your class tell you, directly and clearly, that they appreciate "what you did for them." Such statements by college students are infrequent but not rare. A student may be very appreciative of your teaching but for one or another reason does not or cannot express those feelings to you. But when a student does express appreciation, it is immensely satisfying. I have often felt that my students thought I did not need to hear their appreciation, a good example of putting teachers into a special category of human being who does not need "reinforcement." That, of course, is what happens in parent-child relationships! *If direct expressions of appreciation are infrequent on the university level, they are very rare in elementary and secondary schools.* On several occasions when I was observing in classrooms where it was obvious the students liked, respected, and appreciated the teacher, I asked the teachers this question: "Can you tell me of a time when any child in this classroom expressed appreciation of *anything* you did?" None of these teachers could remember such an instance, although all of them asserted that they knew how positively the students felt toward them. One teacher said with a very puzzled facial expression, "Isn't it strange that none of my students has put his or her feelings into words?" It is strange, but let us remember that such an absence of directness is by no means uncharacteristic of social relationships *in our society.*

Satisfaction from direct expression of appreciation should not be counted on by the public school teacher, however much that teacher may need and want such expressions. It is understandable—is it ever understandable!—if a teacher needs and wants such expressions, in light of the obvious fact that a teacher is *always giving* of him- or herself. But anyone contemplating a career in teaching should not count on such expressions. What that teacher has to be sensitive to are the many indirect signs of appreciation, affection, and respect. And, no less importantly, the teacher has to guard against the tendency to inhibit or lessen his or her direct expressions of appreciation as a reaction to the lopsided disparity to "giving and getting." In general, people vary tremendously in their need for praise, appreciation, and affection. It is the fate of teachers (and parents?) that they cannot count on having that need satisfied by the direct expressions of their students. A distinction is made between intrinsic and extrinsic rewards or satisfactions. What keeps a teacher going are the satisfactions from literally seeing signs of personal and intellectual change in students, and the security in the feeling that in some inchoate, inexpressible way, you are appreciated *at the same time you are taken for granted.* Again I have to say that teaching is not for everybody. That is no criticism or derogation of those for whom teaching may be an inappropriate profession. It is a way of emphasizing that in choosing a career, the match between role and personal needs deserves serious scrutiny.

One other type of occurrence kept me going in teaching. From time to time, I would get a letter from a student, usually several years after he or she was a student, telling me that *now* he or she understands what I was trying to get across in class. Those letters engendered two reactions. The first was to reinforce all my doubts about my capacity to bridge the gap between what I knew and what students could or would comprehend. And I can assure the reader that those doubts never left me, despite such letters. The other reaction, immensely satisfying, was that "it was all worthwhile." And it is! Here are analogues of the letters that teachers have related to me.

1. On the last day of school, some students will ask plaintively, "Can I have you as my teacher next year?"
2. At the beginning of the school year, some students will make it their business to visit their previous teacher's classroom to say hello, a hello expressive of strong feeling.
3. It is infrequent but not rare that a student who was graduated from high school and went off to college will visit one of his or her teachers during a vacation break "just to stay in touch." Several years ago, I developed a friendship with Ed Myers, a retired high school chemistry teacher. One day he was telling me about a student he had in class fifteen years ago. The student had called to arrange a time they could visit together. "He calls me every now and then." As he was relating the work this former student was now doing, it dawned on me that he had told me similar stories about many others of his former students. It is probably the case that Ed is unusual in terms of the number of former students who stay in touch, but in my conversations with other high school teachers, I have gotten similar stories.

Granted that the absolute number of such contacts between student and teacher is not large, they do illustrate the
too neglected point that the number of students who
appreciate a teacher, who have been positively influenced
by that teacher, is larger than the absence of direct expressions would suggest.

Why am I emphasizing the significance of the relative
absence of direct expressions of appreciation of the teacher?
Because unlike others in human service professions (for example,
physicians, lawyers, social workers, psychotherapists), who work
with people who have brought them their personal problems and
who are grateful for whatever help has been rendered, teachers
relate to students on a different basis; that is, a basis that does not
(necessarily) require expressions of gratitude. Why those expressions are so infrequent is less important here than the fact that
they are infrequent. A teacher "needs" such expressions; a
teacher needs to feel his or her efforts are appreciated. But a
teacher also needs to understand that the infrequency of such
expressions cannot be taken personally. A teacher has to have
that sense of inner security not only that his or her efforts have
had the desired effects but also that in some inchoate way—and
it is not always inchoate—students appreciate the teacher's
efforts. That is asking a lot of teachers, but that is the fate of
teachers (and parents). Students expect to be appreciated by
their teachers for what they do and are. So do teachers, who, let
us not forget, are quite human. You would criticize a teacher
who did not express appreciation for what students do and are.
But you would not criticize students who, for one or another
reason, cannot, do not know how, or feel uncomfortable putting
into words the equivalent of "I appreciate what you have done

for me." If you are the kind of person who needs more than students can express, teaching may not be for you. If you are the kind of person who takes satisfaction from arranging, contributing to, and observing the personal and intellectual growth of young people, teaching can be a very satisfying experience.

Are parents a source of appreciation and satisfaction? The answer is yes and no, and it is very complicated. Most parents whose children are developing satisfactorily in school are far more likely to thank God than to thank the teacher. Again, it is not that they are unappreciative but rather that you are being taken for granted; that is, you know your job, and you are doing it well, but going out of their way to say that unambiguously and sincerely is not as frequent as it should be. Why that is so is puzzling (to me), but one reason is that parents, like too many other people, simply have the most superficial comprehension of the complexity a teacher has to manage. Too many people, like too many of those contemplating a career in teaching, have an oversimplified grasp of what it means to teach a group of students each of whom is unique and to each of whom a teacher is supposedly objective and effective. But when parents tell a teacher that they are appreciative of what he or she contributed to their children, it is no end satisfying. It keeps you going.

It is no secret that when a parent is asked to come and talk with a teacher, the parent expects to hear bad news. That is an important fact, because it suggests that the failure of teachers to go out of *their* way personally to express their appreciation of a parent's child—which is a way of expressing appreciation of the parent's rearing of the child—does not reinforce the expression by the parent of whatever appreciation he or she has for the teacher. Parents, no less or more than teachers, have need of appreciation. They, like teachers, do not want to be taken for granted. I have said earlier that the conventional image of a teacher is of a person with students in an encapsulated classroom in an encapsulated school. That image obscures the opportunities a teacher has to develop personal relationships with parents that can be very satisfying *and* instructive to teacher, parents, and child. But as a teacher, *you* will have to take the initiative, because parents tend to view teachers with a strange and inhibiting mixture of respect, fear, and ambivalence. And teachers tend to view parents as uninterested or hypersensitive and judgmental. But when these kinds of attitudinal hurdles are overcome, the satisfactions are real and sustaining. They are sources of satisfaction not available to college professors!

Are you the kind of person who does not take kindly to criticism (explicit or implicit) or challenges to your way of thinking and acting? That is an important question anyone contemplating a career in teaching should not avoid confronting, because there will be parents (and students!) who have the courage and feel the obligation to disagree with what you say and do. If you are the kind of person who will bristle at such challenges, who will be unduly defensive, or who will respond with "who are *you* to tell *me* I am wrong," you may win the battle and completely lose the war. For my purposes here, the validity of the challenge is not relevant. The parent or student may be right or wrong, appropriately or inappropriately articulating his or her opinions. The task of the teacher is to understand, not to "win," to stand one's ground, not to crush the "opponent," to sustain and deepen the relationship, not to terminate it, to be grateful that the challenge is out in the open, not boiling volcanolike underground. In the previous chapter, I asked you to examine yourself in regard to how you view, experience, and manage power-authority. It should be obvious that that is a theme that is never far from the core of a teacher's consciousness. Satisfactions from teaching very much depend on the match between what you are as a person and the demands and obligations of the role. Teaching is not for everybody. It is a fascinating and demanding personal, interpersonal, intellectual process that can be no end rewarding *when done well*, that is, when the needs and goals of the vested interests of all concerned are respected, not violated or derogated. I applaud anyone who, reading what I have said and having engaged in self-scrutiny, decides against teaching as a career. Choosing a career is too important a decision to gloss over what you are as a person. And teaching is too important a societal function to go along with the fiction that teaching is other than one of the most demanding, challenging, trying, satisfying of experiences.

The reader may be surprised to hear that what I am saying to those contemplating a career in teaching is precisely what I would say to anyone thinking of a medical career. In recent decades, the medical community has been the object of criticisms not dissimilar to those directed to the educational one: physicians are not as caring and compassionate as they should be; they are a closed, self-protective, self-serving community; too frequently they make unilateral decisions as if patients were too ignorant to be consulted; they arrogate undue power-authority to themselves and do not react with grace to challenges to their power-authority. What these criticisms suggest—and what many medical educators have been saying for a long time—is that too many people seeking a medical career have a most inadequate comprehension of what a physician encounters in the role of "healer." They are victims of the popular image of a physician as a diagnoser and treater of bodies or symptoms, not of a person with needs, expectations, fears, and questions.

Matters are not helped any by the brute fact that the criteria employed for admission to medical school have nothing to do with personality style. A physician may possess a great deal of knowledge, a teacher may know his or her subject matter, but there is more to treating and teaching than what we ordinarily mean by *knowledge*. And it is that "more" that cannot be left out of the career decision either by the individual or by the program selecting candidates.

I confess that I react very negatively when I hear physicians complain about demanding, or unappreciative, or noncompliant patients, just as I react when I hear similar complaints by teachers about this or that student or this or that parent. Why should that be surprising to either of them? What did they know or expect when they chose their careers? What permitted them to envision a career devoid of all the fascinations and challenges that derive from, as one teacher aptly said, "messing" with the lives of others? It was the same teacher who, after a very trying session with a father, which ultimately was very satisfying, said to me, "So what else is new?"

Satisfactions derive from many sources and are determined by many factors, among the most important of which is the match between your understanding of your interests, assets, and vulnerabilities, on the one hand, and the diverse features of the professional role you choose, on the other. There is much you must and can learn about those features, but the harder task is what you have to face in yourself; that is, the kind of person you are and want to be. Granted that at this stage of your life you cannot be expected to learn all you need to know or to have as secure an understanding of yourself as would be ideally possible. But you have no alternative to persist in seeking knowledge and increased understanding of yourself.

Let us in the next chapter turn to satisfactions one can expect from colleagues. Why is teaching regarded as a "lonely profession"? What will or should be a teacher's obligation to dilute that sense of loneliness? Here again we shall be dealing with two questions. What are the realities of teaching? How can teachers begin to change those realities? We are living at a time when, as never before, our schools and school personnel are objects of concern and change. It is safe to assume that in the next decade or two, our schools will have changed in discernible ways. There are and will be turmoil, controversy, and hot debates. Change should never be confused with progress. I say that because I believe—and this will sound strange to your ears—that the current clamor for change hardly speaks to the nature and dynamics of teaching. The educational community has, in my opinion, done a poor job of helping the public comprehend the complexity of teaching and the characteristics of the social context necessary if that complexity is to be productively exploited. The time is past when teachers could afford to remain passive objects of change. Yes, we expect teachers to give their all to the growth and development of students. *But a teacher cannot sustain such giving unless the conditions exist for the continued growth and development of the teacher.* If only for reasons of self-interest, the teacher has to be an active, assertive agent in fostering those conditions without which routinization of thought and practice subverts professional growth and development. And again I have to say that that is not peculiar to the profession of teaching. The grass is not greener (certainly not *that* much greener) elsewhere. Anyone beginning a career in teaching is entering at a time when he or she can make a difference. But that difference will not be made by passive teachers. Let me flesh out that call for assertiveness.

chapter 6

SATISFACTION
FROM COLLEAGUES

*i*n 1966, my colleagues and I at
the Yale Psycho-Educational Clinic wrote a rather thick book
about our experiences in schools.* There was one chapter in that
book that caused a number of teachers around the country to
write us their appreciation of the contents of that chapter, which
was written by Dr. Murray Levine. The chapter's title was
"Teaching Is a Lonely Profession." That title reflected the
obvious fact that for most of each teaching day, a teacher is with
people who are much younger than he or she. However satisfying
that can be, it is no substitute for being with peers; that is, with
others with whom you can "be" in ways impossible with
children. For example, one teacher said to me, "When I was
home raising my child, there were times, many times, I felt I had
it up to my ears and felt alone. But I could pick up the phone and
call a friend or my neighbor or my husband, or someone: another
adult with whom I could be myself. Now that I am teaching, I
can't pick up the phone and talk to another grown-up." That was
from a teacher who loved her students, who really put out for

* Sarason, S. B., Levine, M., Goldenberg, T., Cherlin, T., and Bennett,
E. *Psychology in Community Settings.* New York: Wiley, 1966.

them, and at the end of the day felt exhausted but satisfied. What she said to me was not a complaint but a statement of the fact that she had need to talk with another adult, someone with whom she could talk about shared experience.

Generally speaking, and the usual exceptions aside, the school day is not organized to allow for discussion with other teachers. There is the break for lunch, of course, but mixing eating with discussion—and let us not confuse chitchat with serious discussion—is understandably not viewed with enthusiasm.

Let me again be briefly autobiographical. My professional background was in clinical psychology, a field in which one seeks to help people with personal problems. The clinician works alone with individual clients and/or their families. But in any clinical facility, there are opportunities to meet with colleagues for the purpose of discussing cases: the nature of problems, the treatment strategy, and outcomes. Those meetings are intended to be learning experiences for everyone in the facility. For me, those meetings were mammothly stimulating and satisfying, if only because they never let me forget (*never* is not too strong) that my view of a particular case was not necessarily shared by my colleagues. They were not brief meetings. Not infrequently, they aroused heated discussion, which, on occasion, had interpersonal repercussions. After all, these meetings were about *theory and practice*, matters about which I and my colleagues had strong opinions. Nevertheless, it would never occur to anyone to suggest that these meetings be eliminated. Indeed, the more meetings, the better. That is why Murray Levine made his priceless quip: "Every clinic should have two staffs: one to attend the meetings and one to do the work." Exaggeration can make a telling point!

When I began to work in classrooms and schools, I was struck by two things. The first was the absence of meetings at which teachers could present, discuss, or just listen to problems of practice. The second was how teachers hungered for and "ate up" rare opportunities to participate in such meetings, especially for individuals relatively new to teaching.

How do we explain the absence in schools of a tradition for such meetings? The answer is a complicated one, beyond the scope of this book. But two parts of the answer can be briefly stated. The first is (again) wrapped up in the conventional image of a teacher: someone in an encapsulated (closed-door) classroom concerned only with students, who has or should have no need to discuss his or her problems of practice with others, who has no *intellectual* need to learn from others or to contribute to the learning of colleagues, who should feel so secure in his or her practices as to make regular meetings with colleagues a wasteful indulgence of precious time. It is an image that accepts and reinforces the "alone" teacher, completely ignoring the sources of a teacher's need to be a member of an intellectual community.

The second part of the answer is that teachers have been self-defeatingly passive in accepting the situation and not taking initiative and responsibility to change this state of affairs. Relevant here is the question, "Why in the late fifties and sixties did teachers join unions, whereas before they vehemently resisted being members of militant unions and seemed content to deal as *single* individuals with those who made school policy?" The answer is that they came to see that they *had* to become more assertive and to give up their passive, "hat-in-hands" approach to officialdom. Unions deal with bread-and-butter issues, and very little with professional issues such as the one I am raising in this chapter.

Why discuss this issue with people who are contemplating a career in teaching? There are probably some people who would argue that I am painting a picture that would dissuade some from deciding to become a teacher. That would be a gross misreading of my intentions. For one thing, one of my purposes and obligations is to alert people making a career decision to important features of that career. No less important—and in some ultimate sense more important—is to emphasize that changing this state of affairs should be a conscious obligation of those entering the field. Put another way, the field will not change unless and until teachers seek to create those conditions the absence of which is a source of dissatisfaction and the presence of which is a source of satisfaction. I am not placing the burden of change only on teachers. Changes elsewhere will be required, but, as in the case of unions, teachers will have to be more active.

I am writing these words during the presidential campaign of 1992. No one who was alive and breathing during that campaign could avoid concluding that pressure for changing our schools is, to indulge in understatement, persistent and strong. All kinds of radical proposals have gained currency and engendered passionate controversy. Perhaps not strangely, teachers' unions and other organizations had very little to say about why too many teachers come to feel so keenly the lack of a sense of belonging to an intellectual community through which they experience stimulation, growth, and mutuality. Teachers, no less than students, have to feel they are alive, interested, and belong. Teachers are inevitably alone with their students, but there is a difference between being alone and feeling lonely. I have come to know schools in which teachers, at least some of them, have exercised leadership to change this state of affairs.

And that is the point: teachers overcame their sense of powerlessness, they accepted responsibility for their own development, they took the initiative to forge new forums through which their need to experience growth and community could be met. Granted, such needs go frequently unmet because of school traditions and the ways in which time is allocated during the school day. But what I saw in these schools underlined a most important point: *teachers are not powerless, and when they face and deal with that point, they derive a degree of satisfaction from their colleagues that adds intellectual and interpersonal zest to their days.* I have known ghetto schools where, despite deplorable and inexcusable physical conditions and inadequate educational materials, the teachers have developed "forums" through which their needs for mutual support and personal-intellectual growth have been so met that most of the teachers passed up opportunities to teach in more aesthetically pleasing, less taxing schools.

That is no argument for schools with deplorable and inexcusable conditions. But it is an argument against the too widely held view that where these conditions are otherwise, teachers will "naturally" find that their needs for mutual support, personal-intellectual growth, and community will be fulfilled. I have known too many suburban, well-heeled schools in which teachers feel these needs are not being met. There are many things money cannot buy, and one of them is the sense that you are continuing to experience the sense of growth with and from children and with and from colleagues. Over the long run, it is those two senses that keep you willingly engaged in your work. If over the long run those conditions do not exist for teachers, those teachers will find it extraordinarily difficult to *sustain* those conditions for their students. *Here again, I must emphasize that this is not peculiar to teaching.* I have known too many professionals in the human service arenas to suggest that the grass is greener elsewhere. It isn't!

Nothing that I have said should be interpreted as suggesting that if teachers became more active (and even militant) in regard to their personal-professional needs, all of the clouds hanging over our schools would disappear and the sun would shine. What will also be required is the recognition by the public and school administrators of the personal-professional needs of teachers. That recognition will be hastened to the degree that teachers exercise more initiative over their professional role and lives.

Why am I saying this to people contemplating a career in teaching? There are two major reasons, and they are inter-related. The more obvious of the two reasons is that unless you take active responsibility for your professional development, unless you protect yourself against the insidious consequences of intellectual-professional loneliness, you reduce the satisfactions you will derive from your career. Let me put it another way. On the "adult" level, a school should not be a collection of individuals in which each teacher takes responsibility only for his or her classroom, in which each teacher feels no special obligation (except to be civil, of course) to and for other teachers, in which teachers have no sense of "family," that sense that, like it or not, your fate is inextricably intertwined with the fate of others, that sense that you *count* in matters crucial to that family. If that is what too many teachers experience, it is *in part* because teachers have been too passive. You could say too *unprofessional,* because one of the defining characteristics of a professional is that he or she *takes* responsibility to create those conditions necessary to discharge obligations to others and oneself in accord with the ideals of the profession.

The second and related reason inheres in the incontrovertible fact that we are living at a time when enormous pressures are being exerted to change schools: their goals, practices, organization, administration, credentialing practices, curricula, autonomy, financing, and more. (It is very similar to what is happening in regard to medical care.) There are two features to this cauldron of advice and change quite relevant to our present discussion. They are features with very different focuses. One reflects the position that teachers are in need of changing what they do in their closed-door classrooms. It would not be unfair to say that these proposals *tell* teachers how they should think and practice in their encapsulated classrooms. Some of these proposals have much merit. The other feature is that teachers have to be given and assume more responsibility in decisions affecting *the entire school*, not only their classrooms. This proposal reflects the *political* principle that those who will be affected by a decision or policy should have other than a token role in the formulation, acceptance, or rejection of that decision. That is the principle that has been applied to environmental matters (for example, building a new nuclear plant, a new factory that will give out noxious gases, a new highway in or near residential areas, the placement of new housing developments, the destruction of architecturally significant structures). In such matters, the day is past when the interests and feelings of relevant parties can be ignored or lightly dismissed. It is a principle that has gained a good deal of currency in discussions about the role of teachers in school governance. It has gained more than currency; it has begun to be taken seriously in practice in some schools. Inherent in the principle is a vision of teachers as a *collegial group* that has input into any decision with an impact on teachers, students, and parents. It is a vision in dramatic contrast to the one of the single teacher in a closed-door classroom, alone and lonely with his or her students and problems, poignantly aware that he or she is powerless in the larger scheme of school life.

It should occasion no surprise that giving teachers more power in school governance has not been enthusiastically greeted by some people. Those who have power should not be expected graciously to decrease or share that power. Nevertheless, there is good reason to believe that in coming years, the principle will be increasingly implemented in schools, and for two reasons. The first is that the general public is sufficiently dissatisfied with the educational outcomes of our schools that they look favorably on proposals for change that give promise of improving those outcomes; that is, they are prepared for changes that are other than cosmetic. The second reason is that the principle has a political and moral compellingness that makes practical sense in that it accords responsibility *and* accountability to those who are truly on the firing line. At the present time, blame for educational ineffectiveness is directed to administrators by teachers, or directed to teachers by administrators, or directed by both to the "system," or to all of those by the community. In this context, accountability is a shifting target enveloped in a dense fog. By according teachers a serious role in decision making—and let us not forget that teachers are by far the most numerous adults in a school—the locus of accountability becomes much more clear.

Here again, some readers contemplating a career in education may have second thoughts because I am describing a changing educational scene that is and will be marked by power struggles. Those readers are seeing the bottle as half-empty. There are those who will see the bottle as half-full because they will be entering the field at an exciting time in which they can make a difference, in which they can contribute to the reform of our schools. The pessimist sees conflicts; the optimist sees opportunities. The pessimist retreats from challenge; the optimist embraces challenge. The pessimist wants to travel a well-paved, pothole-free career highway; the optimist wants to repave that highway.

I am in no way derogating the pessimist or giving brownie points to the optimist. I used those labels in order to suggest (again) that confronting "who you are"—the kinds of situations in which you feel comfortable, the satisfactions you need and want, your reactions to conflict and frustration, the quality of interpersonal relationships you seek—requires that you ask whether predictable features of a career in teaching are, so to speak, up your alley. Anyone who is now beginning a career in teaching should be prepared to expect ups and downs, professional highs and lows, satisfactions and disappointments, the sense of personal-intellectual growth and the sense that the world is against you. We are not living in easy times, and saying that in regard to education is an indulgence in understatement.

What happens in our schools in coming decades will in part be determined by the characteristics, personal and professional, of those who enter teaching. Unless and until those entering teaching have a clear and firm sense of responsibility for changing life in school, for how life should be lived with students and colleagues, for one's role as a professional who has ideas, opinions, values, and goals that deserve a respectful hearing—when that sense of responsibility becomes second nature to teachers, schools stand a chance of changing in desirable ways. Teachers are not important, they are crucial. For too long, teachers have accepted a lowly position in the hierarchy of power. That is changing (too slowly) and will continue to change. Calls for such change come largely from sources external to our schools. That is necessary but not sufficient. The change must also come from internal sources, and that means teachers. It is a glimpse of the obvious to say that teachers should feel a responsibility for the students in their classrooms. It is also a glimpse of the obvious— albeit one hard for some people to see—that that responsibility is mightily influenced by decisions made by others in the school or "downtown," decisions about which teachers had no input, engendering in them a sense of unworthiness and aloneness. Is it any wonder that many teachers have little sense of allegiance and responsibility to the school as an independent family? That, I have said, is changing, and the pace of that change will be determined by the efforts of teachers to change the quality of professional life in their schools. The challenge, I know, is daunting, but the payoff, personal and institutional, can be enormously gratifying. Teaching has to become a social profession, not a lonely one. There is too much at stake for it to be otherwise. If, in light of what I have said, teaching "calls" you, you will not be disappointed.

I have emphasized that the person contemplating a career in teaching has to take at least two types of initiatives: to look into yourself and the kind of person you are, and to talk with people who have had diverse experiences and roles in public education. In the next chapter, that emphasis becomes center stage as I try to convince you that you know a good deal about learning, classrooms, teachers, and schools. You are far from ignorant about some of the most important issues in the ongoing controversy about improving our schools. I know that you see yourself as the opposite of an expert. It is not my purpose to confer on you the label of expert. If you are understandably not an expert, it does not mean you are without crucially relevant knowledge.

chapter 7

YOU KNOW MORE THAN YOU THINK AND MORE THAN THEY GIVE YOU CREDIT FOR

My goal in this chapter is to convince you that its title has validity. That is important for at least two major reasons. In the previous chapters, I emphasized that because of your inexperience and lack of relevant knowledge, you must make every effort to seek and digest as much knowledge as possible about what a career in teaching will require of you. That advice still holds good. You do have "deficits" in knowledge, but, as I shall endeavor to persuade you, you have some crucially important "assets" in experience that you should mine. You are far from being an ignoramus! The other major reason is that not only should your experiential assets enter into your decision, but once you have decided on such a career, you must use those assets as a basis for judging how well what you will be asked to learn in a preparatory program helps you make sense of those experiential assets. What you must avoid is falling into the trap of passively accepting attitudes about and conceptions of a teacher's role that conflict with your experience. I am not suggesting that you be argumentative with your college teachers but rather that you be true to yourself—that is, you will not lightly dismiss or forget or give up conclusions you came to as a student who spent twelve years in elementary, middle, and high school. Those conclusions inevitably will contain errors of different sorts, but they will also contain some important truths.

You owe it to yourself to listen to and reflect upon what you will be taught, but not at the expense of giving up all you have *learned about learning* in those twelve years. Some college teachers have the understandable but still inexcusable tendency to view students as having empty heads that need to be filled. As a college teacher, it took me years to realize that I vastly underestimated what students knew. After all, I was teaching *psychology,* and on what basis was I assuming that my students had empty psyches, that they had not had experiences directly relevant to what naive I assumed would be for them completely new knowledge? If I say such a stance is understandable, it is in large part because my students presented themselves as if they had no experiential assets I could or should exploit. And that is the point: students too readily assumed that they had no basis for using their experience to question in any way the "truths" I was giving them. When teacher and students collude in accepting that assumption, it is a recipe for nonproductive learning.

Teachers teach and students learn! Productive learning occurs when students and teachers teach each other. Teachers do know more than students, but unless that more takes into account what students know and have experienced, the students are robbed of the opportunity of examining, critiquing, and enlarging their personal and intellectual horizons. In the course of your professional education, you will frequently hear the maxim "You teach children, not subject matter." That maxim is intended to emphasize that you be sensitive to "what and where children are." Teaching should always deal with two subject matters: the world of the learner and the content and structure of the subject matter. That maxim is as valid for the individual in a teacher preparatory program as it is for a first-grade child. Too frequently, it is a maxim honored more in the breach than in the practice.

Let us start with the first major reason justifying this chapter's title, and let us do so by asking this question: When you review your twelve years as a student, which teachers come quickly to mind? Let me personally answer the question. Because I am undoubtedly a very senior citizen, I have to point out that the teachers I remember now are the same teachers I remembered when I was much younger. For example, when I was in graduate school—approximately six or seven years after being graduated from high school—a number of my student colleagues and I were discussing the nature of memory, in the course of which someone suggested that each of us write down the names of the teachers we had in our public school days. We were quite surprised at the relative shortness of our lists. (We could recall in our mind's eye several teachers whose names could not be dredged up.)

My list then was what it is today, and in this order: Miss Stephenson, Mr. Coleman, Miss Collins, Mr. Triest, Mr. Hunkins, Mrs. Schweig, Mr. McDonald. The last two names were not teachers. Mr. McDonald was the principal of my elementary (K–8) school, and Mrs. Schweig was the assistant principal. But they were unforgettable because I and others viewed them as fearsome, punishing, if not child-devouring. The fact is that I can recall not a single instance when I interacted in any way with either of them, and I can recall no instance when I saw them in any way punish or discipline a child. But to the children in that school, Mr. McDonald and Mrs. Schweig were to be avoided like the plague. If you were in the hall and you saw either of them, your heartbeat mightily escalated, especially if they appeared to be approaching you. Why are they, who were not my teachers, on my list? For one thing, I cannot think of my elementary school days without their images being conjured up. I *feared* them. For all I know, they may have been lovely, decent, sensitive, supportive people, but you couldn't prove that by my testimony or that of my classmates. They never did or said anything to give students the feeling that they could be trusted. There is a difference between fear and respect. We *feared* them. We saw them as seeing us as potential criminals. We loved and respected Tom Kelly, the police officer who directed traffic at the busy intersection where the school was located. He was a delightful, friendly, joking, lovable person. When he was killed by a car at that intersection, we cried. If that had happened to Mr. McDonald or Mrs. Schweig, we probably would have been sad, but we would not have cried.

Why do I start with Mr. McDonald and Mrs. Schweig? For one thing, I wish to emphasize that how a child views an adult in the school may be dramatically discrepant with how that adult intends or would like to be viewed. I have no doubt whatsoever that Mr. McDonald and Mrs. Schweig did not want to be feared. But I can recall nothing said by either of them or any of my teachers to change my basic stance of fear, my belief that if they approached me, I was in trouble. (It was not until I was an adult that I learned that that is precisely what many parents believe: if they are asked to come to see the principal, they are going to hear bad news. Parents are not accustomed to being summoned to school to be told good news.) The more general point I wish to make is that young children, *like everyone else*, form impressions of others less on the basis of what they say or do not say and more (much more) on what they experience in their give-and-take with others. And by *experience*, I mean circumscribed instances in which the needs, expectations, and goals of a child are positively or negatively affected by the words and actions of an adult. It is not that actions speak louder than words but that actions are incomparably more fateful than words. I may very well have been told that Mr. McDonald and Mrs. Schweig were not to be feared, but there was nothing in my personal experience to lead me to change my mind. Fear is the enemy of trust, and trust is the interpersonal vehicle by means of which different personal worlds can begin to overlap. I had absolutely no basis for trusting Mr. McDonald and Mrs. Schweig.

As I have looked back and replayed my school days on my internal video screen, there were very few teachers I can say I trusted. Let me hasten to add that I never feared a teacher the way I did Mr. McDonald and Mrs. Schweig. Why, then, were there so few whom I did trust? Why when I think of trust do I think only of Mr. Coleman and Miss Stephenson? One reason is that I believed they were interested not only in my academic performance but in *me*; that is, what I thought and felt. When I gave a wrong answer to a question, they did not say "That is wrong" and call on another student. They tried to determine why and how I arrived at the wrong answer. And they did that calmly, patiently, as if I had piqued their curiosity, which they had to satisfy. With other teachers, I would not volunteer an answer unless I was *absolutely*, 100 percent sure my answer was correct. With Mr. Coleman and Miss Stephenson, I was relaxed and not fearful of appearing stupid. In fact, I enjoyed those give-and-take interactions. Their classes were interesting, they asked us interesting, even puzzling questions, they challenged us to draw on our out-of-class experience. And in doing so, they did one other thing: they revealed why and how *they* thought as they did. We learned a lot about them as people. If I had to put in one sentence what has stayed with me from their classes, it would go like this: "There is more than one way to think about and solve a problem."

When I think of these two people (they were more than the label *teacher* conventionally conjures up), the word *fair* always comes to mind. That is a hard word to define briefly. For my present purposes, let me just say that it appeared as if who you were, and how "smart" you were, were never grounds for ignoring or devaluing you. Regardless of who and what you were—and the students were very heterogeneous on any variable you can name—you *counted*.

Let me now tell you about Miss Collins, whom I had in the ninth grade and who influenced my life. She did not have the "open," challenging style of Miss Stephenson or Mr. Coleman. I never felt I knew her or that she was particularly interested in me other than as a performing student. She was a prim, constricted, low-key, curriculum-oriented woman who in her quiet way ran a quiet class. If she rarely smiled or expressed any strong feeling, she was not intimidating. She taught Latin. In those days (shortly after the Civil War!), you took Latin if you were college-bound. You would be right if you assumed that students took Latin with the same enthusiasm they took a horrible tasting medicine. For the first month of class, it was all medicine. Then, slowly but steadily, Miss Collins began to demonstrate how some of the words we used every day derived from Latin. To me and a few other students, it came as a revelation that English mightily derived and developed from Latin. Yes, it was a Latin class, but to me it was also a class in the English language, *my* language. It was Miss Collins who stimulated us to look upon a dictionary as a kind of detective story. If Miss Collins was not an interpersonally interesting teacher, she was an intellectually mind-expanding teacher. She made "dead" Latin personally "alive."

Now to Mr. Hunkins and Mr. Triest (and many others whose names I cannot recall). The first word that comes to mind is *uninteresting*. Not only were they uninterested in me (or any other student), but they did not seem interested in *anything*, including the subject matter. It is as if they came to a class with a recipe (= lesson plan) that said "Do this first, that second, and that third, and if you follow instructions, you will end up with a palatable dish you will enjoy." There was nothing to enjoy! We were treated and felt like robots. More correctly, it is as if we had empty heads and hearts. The fact is that a lot was going on in my head and heart, but God forbid that I should put it into words. My job was to learn what I was told to learn even though in my "unformed" mind, I knew there was a difference between learning and understanding. And I learned one other thing: even if I learned but did not understand, do not ask questions, do not reveal your stupidity, do not ask "why" questions, do not take up valuable teacher time. By conventional standards, I was a "good" learner. By my own standards, I was a very poor understander. The classroom was no place to seek or expect to gain understanding. It was a place to get good grades, to appear as if you understood, not a place to ask questions that nobody else seemed to have (which, of course, was not true), but a place in which you had better be able to answer the seemingly scores of questions the teacher asked. None of these teachers *invited* questions. On the contrary, they made you feel that if you asked questions, you were either stupid or a show-off. None of the teachers responded to questions the way Miss Collins did. I said she was prim, low-key, undemonstrative of feeling. But when you asked her a question about whether a particular word in English derived from Latin, her eyes took on an excited cast, an ever so small smile seemed to struggle for expression, and she helped you to answer your question. I can sum up by saying that in these other classrooms, productive learning was defined by the number of questions I could answer, how well I could regurgitate what I was supposed to learn. That definition does contain a kernel of truth, but only a kernel. Another way of summing up is to say that the bulk of my classrooms were uninteresting, boring, and without much point.

Why do Mr. Triest and Mr. Hunkins stand out in my memory? Why do I remember their names and not those of similar teachers for whom subject matter was infinitely more important than what was going on in our hearts and minds? The answer is that I did not respect them. There were many teachers who were riveted on subject matter, but in some inchoate way, I concluded that they cared about the subject matter, if not about us. Mr. Triest and Mr. Hunkins, I and others had to conclude, cared about nothing except getting through class without once getting up from their chairs. Their classes were ones in which nothing seemed to make sense. Mr. Hunkins taught introductory chemistry, Mr. Triest introductory German. We ended up having no respect for or interest in Mr. Triest, Mr. Hunkins, chemistry, or German. There are people today who assert that the level of learning in a classroom is largely affected by factors extrinsic to the classroom, for example, family socioeconomic status. They never had the likes of Mr. Triest and Mr. Hunkins!

I could go on and on, but I do not see the point. I have

revealed enough to buttress the conclusion that by the time I finished high school, I had had experiences quite relevant to conceptions of what makes life in a classroom interesting and challenging or boring and even deadly. Needless to say, I did not know that I had learned a lot about the ingredients working for and against productive learning. I was *just* a high school graduate. It could never occur to me that I had experiential assets relevant to matters educational. Who was I to pass judgment on teachers, classrooms, and the nature of learning? Is there any doubt whatsoever that my teachers would view me as without assets on the basis of which I was justified to come to conclusions? If after high school I had entered a teacher preparatory program—and in those days, you could do just that—it would have been with the attitude that nothing in my school years was of value in learning to become a teacher. I would have looked at my college teachers from precisely the same stance from which I had looked at my public school teachers: I knew nothing, they knew it all; their job was to pour in, mine was to absorb; I had only deficits, they would provide me assets; they were entitled to opinions because they had experience, I was not so entitled because I lacked experience.

What do you come up with when you review your school years? Which teachers stand out and why? Who turned you on or off? In which classes did you find yourself *willingly* eager to learn more? How frequent were boredom, lack of interest, and pointlessness? On which teachers would you confer sainthood because in some way or other you now know that something about what they were as teachers and/or people rang a bell you still hear? Is what I related about my school years (which were well over sixty years ago!) markedly different from what you recall? That there will be differences among us can be taken for granted. But are those differences of such a degree as to cause you to disagree with these statements:

1. In too many of our classrooms, children rarely, sometimes never, have what I will for the sake of brevity call a mind-expanding experience.
2. In too many of our classrooms, the structure and ambience do not encourage children to give voice to their questions about subject matter, personal experience, and the world they live in. Put another way, children live in two worlds, and the twain shall never meet.
3. From the standpoint of the student, there is no separation between what is being taught and who is teaching it. To the student, the teacher is a person whose words and actions determine whether or not he or she will feel understood, fairly judged, valued, encouraged, as someone who counted, someone whose feelings and needs are not taken for granted, someone who wants to feel *interpersonally safe* to be expressive, spontaneous, even probing and "wrong."
4. Teachers, *all* of your teachers, contributed to your admittedly vague sense of the ingredients that make for productive learning. And that sense is always based on a comparison, a contrast between a Miss Stephenson and a Mr. Hunkins.

The point is not whether you find yourself agreeing with all, part, or none of these statements but rather that you have had valuable experience relevant to learning about learning (which is always social in nature). You do have assets. So, if you are contemplating a career in teaching, it should not be from the stance that you will be entering a completely new world for which you have no personal compass. That does not mean that these assets are a form of hands-on-the-Bible truths that will not require amending, enlarging, recasting. But it does mean that you know where you stand and what you stand for and that you will not easily give up your beliefs because someone says you are wrong. Your beliefs came from your experience, and you should change those beliefs on the basis of new experience and not because someone *says* you are mistaken. Your obligation to yourself and your teachers is to listen, to "hear" what they say, to reflect on it, not passively to assume that the voice of authority requires submission. Productive learning is a struggle, a willing struggle from which comes a sense of change and growth. It makes no difference whether you are a first-grader or someone entering a teacher preparation program. Productive learning has its joys, but they are a consequence of intellectual and personal struggle.

This chapter had a goal beyond trying to convince you that you have valuable assets. If I have, in part at least, been convincing, you will then better understand why being a teacher is among the most constructively impactful roles there are. *If you can do for your students what your best teacher did for you in the ways he or she did it, you will have justified your professional existence.* Your goal is not to become *a* teacher but to become one consistent with the personal style and intellectual creativity of those teachers whom you have cause to remember with gratitude.

It is easy to say "be true to yourself." Like all clichés, that saying contains a kernel of truth. The problem is to determine what you mean by "yourself." What I have endeavored to do in this chapter (and previous ones) is to suggest that in regard to becoming a teacher, "yourself" is, among other things, a condensation of attitudes, perceptions, and values forged in years of experience that led you, albeit vaguely, to define the conditions in which *you* came alive, in contrast to those in which *you* were going through the motions. *You* know when "yourself" was and is engaged. It is that engagement that you owe to your students. It is not a matter of imitation. It is a matter of personal-intellectual-professional *development*, and I italicize that word in order to make the obvious point that however clear the image of your best teachers is in your mind's eye, you are a unique individual who will have to find your own way to be true to that image. As a teacher, I undoubtedly looked quite different from Miss Stephenson, Mr. Coleman, and Miss Collins. I would like to believe that whatever my style, it reflected what these teachers stood for and did for me. If I was not the superb teacher they were, I have never forgotten what the best is. And if I have never forgotten that, I never have forgotten my worst teachers, who, in a strange way, were very impactful on my developing self.

chapter 8

THE TEACHER OF WHOM?

*i*f there is anything I learned in my decades of teaching psychology graduate students—and for several years I taught medical students—it is that many students change their minds about the area in which they want to specialize or the client population they wish to serve. It was not infrequent that they changed their minds by the middle of the first year of professional preparation. The medical student who had visions of performing complicated surgery may have given up those fantasies for any number of reasons. The law student who was intent on a career in corporate law may have decided that the logic, beauty, and complexity of constitutional law would be more interesting over the lifetime. The psychology student who was going to major in experimental psychology may have found that he or she was more interested in child development. These changes were not only frequent but often unsettling. Not infrequently, the individuals felt guilty that they wanted to make a new choice; that is, it said something negative about how mature they were.

It is hard to make a generalization about the why of these changes, but one contributing factor was obvious: almost from day one of their professional preparation they were exposed—via faculty, other students, and required readings—to a variety of career possibilities, and in ways that caused them to reflect about their initial choice. There is nothing like new knowledge and experience to challenge the stability of a career choice, which is the reason I have urged you actively to seek relevant new knowledge and experience before you make a final choice. The other reason is that far from feeling any guilt about changing your mind, you should be prepared for more than one change. I will have more to say about this later in this chapter.

Those who contemplate a career in teaching have some idea about whom they would like to teach. Some may wish to teach elementary or middle school children, others see themselves as high school teachers, still others find themselves drawn to early childhood education, and there are those who wish to teach children in special education (mentally retarded, emotionally disturbed, or physically handicapped children). Unlike the kinds of professional preparatory programs with which I have been primarily associated—where students early on are exposed to, even plunged into, a variety of experiences in a variety of sites— preparatory programs for educators rarely provide such career-determining opportunities. Once you decide on the type of child you wish to teach, you enter a program concentrating on that kind of child. You do not enter that program on the basis of having sampled, however briefly and even superficially, what teaching may be like with another type of child. And having entered that program, there will be no opportunity for sampling outside that program.

There is nothing "wrong" with this state of affairs as long as you confront and accept two assumptions. The first is that the choice was made on valid personal, experiential, reasoned grounds. That is asking a lot of a young person contemplating a career choice, which is why I have been urging you actively to seek knowledge and experience (again however brief and superficial) that will afford you a *comparative* basis for your choice. *That advice holds regardless of whether you contemplate a career in education, law, medicine, social work, or psychology.* You do not make such a decision sitting in an armchair indulging your thoughts, hopes, expectations, and fantasies. There is too much at stake to bypass the energetic seeking of knowledge, experience, and counsel. I have known too many professionals outside of education who berated themselves for their failure "better to learn what I was getting into." It may interest you to know that over the decades, I came to know a fair number of Yale undergraduates who decided almost at birth that they wanted to be physicians, never for an instance contemplated an alternative, became physicians, and later came to regret (to some degree, at least) their choice. It may be that I heard only from those who had some regret. That in no way undercuts my point that *you* have to assume the responsibility to learn as much as you can, not only about your choice of career but about the type of child you want to teach.

Permit me to assume that you agree with me. That assumption allows me to return to a point I made earlier in this book, which I will now put in the form of a question: What is your responsibility to your profession? If you believe as I do that anyone in a teacher preparatory program should have *some* opportunity to experience the nature of life with and the teaching of the major categories of children (from early childhood to high school students), is it not your responsibility *when you become a full-fledged professional* to advocate for such opportunities? This book is for those who may choose a career in teaching. What I am saying here is that you are entering a field via preparatory programs that are in need of change, and *you* can play a role in bringing about such change. Indeed, that is what I find so challenging and even exciting about a career in teaching. *You* can play a role in that change, but only if *you* know what you stand for and why.

Changes in professional education come about in two ways: strong pressures from sources external to the field and, as importantly, from internal sources. We are living at a time when the external pressures for educational change are persistent and strong. They will not go away; if anything they will grow stronger. It is the internal pressures that have to become stronger, and among the most important of those internal pressures have to be teachers. When you become a professional teacher, you have taken on the obligation to do what you can on the basis of what you believe to improve your profession. Yes, you have an obligation to do for students what *your* best teachers did for you. But you also have the obligation to improve your profession. You are a single individual, but you are part of by far the largest professional group in education.

For more than two decades, I actively participated in special education preparatory programs. Let me briefly state some of my observations and conclusions:

1. When my participation began, special education meant special classes, which also meant that teachers and students in these classes were, so to speak, walled off from the rest of the school. The unverbalized assumption seemed to be that these classes had unique students requiring unique under-standing by uniquely educated teachers. That assumption was not only invalid, it was nonsense. But what was not

nonsense but quite unfortunate was that the students who entered the program had done so because they had already accepted the assumption. There was no opportunity in the program that would allow them to begin to see that the assumption was not divinely inspired, that teaching "regular" and "special" students was not dramatically different. We (Burton Blatt and I) had difficulty convincing students that most of what we were telling them contradicted the assumption. And why should they be convinced? They had no experience in a regular classroom of any kind.

2. At the same time that I was participating in the special education program, I was conducting research in elementary and middle schools, where it was immediately obvious that regular class teachers saw special classes as mysterious, isolated places where little resembling teaching went on. In fact, all but a few teachers had never set foot in a special class in their school. Needless to say, none of them had ever had a course relevant to special education. When asked, they would say that they never had experience with the types of children in special classes, even though they would conclude otherwise if they had had the opportunity to observe a special class for only a day.

3. I was driven to the conclusion that the failure of teachers to have had some exposure to the major categories of children found in our schools reinforced invalid assumptions, worked against a sense of collegiality, and robbed teachers of the opportunity to alter their beliefs.

4. I was also driven to the conclusion that regular teachers could not believe that teaching special class children could be no less challenging, interesting, and productive than teaching those they taught. Put another way: children in

these classes were devoid of the feelings, needs, and strivings "regular" children had, and they were incapable of learning and changing.*

5. I encouraged one of my graduate students to do a study about how regular class teachers viewed their kindergarten colleagues, and vice versa. The results were unambiguous: they saw each other as existing in two different worlds, each having unique knowledge, methods, and goals. Regular teachers tended to see kindergarten teachers as several levels beyond babysitters; that is, not *real* teachers. This judgment was one of which kindergarten teachers were quite aware.

What is the relevance of this for those contemplating a career in teaching and trying to decide which type of child you wish to teach? For one thing, it should sensitize you to the possibility that you are eliminating possible choices not on some comparative, experiential basis but rather on, to put it baldly, ignorance or inexperience or both. That is especially the case for the individual who finds him- or herself saying, "I don't want to teach preschoolers and kindergartners because that is not *real* teaching," or "Teaching handicapped children would be too depressing, and, besides, the academic payoff is small."

I suppose I say what I do because my first professional job was in an institution for mentally retarded people. I took that

---

* In 1975, Congress passed Public Law 94-142, which was intended (among other things) to drastically reduce the number of handicapped children *not* in a regular classroom. This has been known as the "mainstreaming" law. It is beyond the scope of this book to say more about 94-142 and its mixed, complicated consequences, except to say that many regular class teachers learned for the first time that regular and special children did not constitute two nonoverlapping human species.

position for several reasons, the most crucial of which was that in undergraduate school, one of my instructors had become ill and his class was taken over by a state employee (a psychologist) responsible for admission of handicapped children to state institutions. We visited these institutions and talked with a variety of personnel. Without that experience, I would have approached that first job with low expectations. As it turned out, that first job forever changed me: my understanding of people, the insidious role of stereotypes and prejudice, the bottomless satisfaction you can experience from treating a person as a person regardless of his or her appearance, IQ, or "strange" ways. Everything I have ever done, researched, and written about in psychology bears the imprint of the four years in that position (despite the fact that the institution was in the middle of the rural Connecticut nowhere).

Now for a telling, instructive point: my friends and colleagues in graduate school thought I was crazy willingly to work with a mentally retarded population. "How can you stand it?" they would ask. "Doesn't it get you down?" Imprisoned as they were in stereotypes and prejudice, they could explain my choice only on grounds that I was a nut. Why should it have been otherwise? Nothing in their experience could serve as a challenge to their beliefs. I gave up trying to explain why I was not the depressed soul they thought I should be.

The five points I made earlier are in another and less obvious way relevant to the choice of type of child you think you will enjoy teaching. Implicit in those points was what I consider to be a fact: *regardless of which category of child you choose, the odds are overwhelming that the children in your class will vary widely and wildly on almost every significant personal, intellectual, and behavioral characteristic.* Of course, high school students are different in obvious ways from middle school students, who are different from elementary school children, who are different from preschoolers (and kindergartners), and each is different from those in special classes or programs. *But in each classroom in each category, the teacher will be confronted with what in principle are identical problems centering around variations in the motivations, learning styles, behavioral styles, likability, curiosities, interests, assets, and deficits of students.*

It makes no difference what type of child you will teach. You will like some and dislike others; some will intrigue you, and some will bore you; some will catch on quickly, and others may never "get it"; some you would like to embrace, and others you would like to slap; some are "smarter" than their IQs suggest, and others are denser than their IQs predicted; some are reflective in temperament, and others are impulsive; some you would like to have year after year, and others you would like to place elsewhere as soon as possible, like yesterday. You may not know it—it is easy to forget—but you will have a good deal in common with teachers of other types of children. Any expectation that because your students will be homogeneous on the basis of IQ, achievement test scores, age, or even family background, you will not be confronted with all kinds of heterogeneity—that expectation you would be well advised to begin to unlearn.

Again, and regardless of the type of child you wish to teach, you, like any conscientious teacher, will be tested; that is, precisely because you have your likes and dislikes, your needs to feel respected and competent, your assets and vulnerabilities, your stereotypes and prejudices, you will agonize over the possibility that you are being unfair or insensitive to some of your students. And there will be times when you will conclude that you were unfair and insensitive. Any teacher who tells you that he or she does not agonize is a person who understands neither self nor students. Agonizing is an expression of interest and puzzlement about the chemistry of social relationships. Agonizing is an admission, a most realistic admission, that you have an obligation to recognize and be sensitive to another person, whom you may or may not like, who puzzles you in some way, who may bring out the worst in you, but to whom you *know* at the core of your being that you "owe" the best you can be and give.

The choice of type of children to teach should never be made on the basis that such children will be "easy" (whatever that may mean). Teaching is never easy, except for teachers incapable of recognizing and adapting to individual differences among children. If you go into teaching, it should be with the knowledge that you will fall short of the mark. *Falling short of the mark is no disgrace. Not knowing what the mark is is a disgrace.*

I have been discussing some of the implications and consequences of the lack of opportunity to sample what life and teaching are like with the major categories of children. Here I wish to interconnect that lack of opportunity to a growing phenomenon in the adult work force (professional or otherwise). I refer to the fact that in the post–World War II era, increasing numbers of people resist and resent performing in the same role over the lifetime, what I call the one-life, one-career imperative: you are taught to expect that having made *a* career choice, you are, so to speak, stuck with that choice. Why many people come to view that imperative with very mixed feelings is beyond the scope of this book. Suffice it to say that many people have a strong need for new challenges, for new ways to build on what they have done and experienced. There are clear, practical obstacles to changing one's career, be it a change within a profession or a change to a very different profession. A contributing factor is the lack of opportunity to sample new roles in new sites. Take, for example, an elementary school teacher who has been a successful one but who would like to teach in a high school or in a special education program or in an early childhood program. In short, that teacher wants to remain a teacher but with a different population of children. That teacher may never have had the opportunity to experience to any degree what life and teaching are like with other kinds of students. Some would advise that teacher to obtain formal credentials that would allow him or her to make a change. If that advice is taken, it involves a good deal of time and money. Should it not be possible for teachers to have sample experience in order to determine whether they wish to make such a serious commitment?

It is obvious from what I have said that I believe that anyone contemplating a career in teaching should make every effort to gain some degree of familiarity with teaching different types of students. What I am now saying is that *after* a person has become a teacher he or she should seek such familiarity, if he or she has the curiosity. I have spent time in two schools (both middle schools) where each year two teachers could, if they wished, teach in the elementary or high school for one semester. They were not required to enter a new preparatory program. What was required of them was a reasoned, convincing case for why such an experience would be personally *and* intellectually productive. I spoke to some of these teachers, each of whom said that it was one of their most invigorating, horizon-expanding, career-altering experiences.

Many people, in our culture at least, have need for new challenging experiences. I have no doubt that that is the case with those contemplating a career in teaching. What I have endeavored to do in this chapter is to urge you not to assume that your decision to become a teacher, and your choice of type of child to teach, will forever satisfy your need for new challenging, personally testing experience. For some of you, that assumption may turn out to be both satisfying and productive. For others, it will be otherwise, and they owe it to themselves to do what they can to change where and whom they teach.

I cannot conclude this chapter without reminding you that what I have discussed is not peculiar to a teaching career. It is no less relevant for those choosing another profession for their lifetime. The logo of my late and lamented travel agent was "See the world before you leave it." The logo of this chapter has been "Experience as much of the world of your profession as you can." If currently there are obstacles to acting consistent with that logo, do you not have a responsibility to advocate for reducing the strength and number of those obstacles? If teachers become powerful advocates in this matter, change becomes a real possibility. The world cannot listen to or hear such advocacy unless teachers forcefully articulate it. Those who enter teaching should do so not only for what they want to do for students but also because of what they want to do for themselves.

chapter *9*

CHANGE, RESISTANCE, AND REFLECTION

i have said that you can count
on death, taxes, and being wrong about something you were
convinced was right, natural, and proper. Now I must add to the
list that beginning at the time of your entry into a teacher
preparatory program, you can count on feeling the need to
change, either because something inside you says you should
change or because the pressure comes from an outside source.
You can truly count on that, which means that when you
experience those internal or external pressures—and sometimes
they occur at the same time—you should not be all that
surprised. People differ markedly in response to such pressure.
In the case of internal pressure, there are people who will view
it as a sign of a personal inadequacy, a kind of defect symptomatic
of a lack of wisdom and maturity, as if they had a view of
themselves as paragons of perfection. There are those who will
rationalize away or downplay the validity of that internal
pressure, as if it is a kind of temporary aberration that one puts
in the file-and-forget category. And then there are those who
accept the significance of the internal pressure but who conclude
that external circumstances work against pursuing change.

There are other reactions I need not list. The point is that these internal pressures are predictable, important, and consequential. They are signs that you are struggling with the dynamics of growth. I deliberately put it in positive terms to emphasize that personal-intellectual-professional growth is a struggle, an opportunity to test and justify one's beliefs and practices. If at this point in your life you were asked if you expected to experience changes in your beliefs, ideas, and ways of acting, you would unhesitatingly answer, "Of course." If you were then asked whether those changes would be associated with struggle, conflict, guilt, and turmoil, would your answer be another unhesitating "Of course"? I have asked both questions of scores of young people in the process of making a career choice (in and out of education), and I have to predict that your answer to the second one would not be an unhesitating "Of course." It is quite likely—I will bet and give you attractive odds—you will be nonplussed, become reflective and even inarticulate! Why that is so is beyond the purposes of this book, which, as I said in an early chapter, is not a psychology text. What I ask you to accept as a fact is that when we in our mind's eye project ourselves into "our" future, we do not envision ourselves as struggling with more or less frequent internal pressures to change in some important ways. And yet those pressures are predictable, even if their substance, strength, occasions, and consequences are not.

What are examples of internal pressures experienced by some teachers? Here are a few:

1. "Why do I have so much trouble managing children who are aggressive with other children? Why do the teachers who previously taught them report they had no special

difficulty? I must be doing something wrong. What should I do differently? How should I change?"

2. "Why is there so little laughter in my classroom? Why do other teachers say that I take myself too seriously, that I do not give them the impression I am enjoying my work? What does that say about me and how I understand myself? How can I learn to be different?"

3. "Why is it that I no longer come to school with the eagerness and anticipation I used to have? What does that mean? Does it mean that I have changed but I was unaware of it? What can I do to change this state of affairs?"

4. "Why is it that when I come away from a meeting with my principal or one of the curriculum supervisors, I am angry with myself because it is so hard for me to tell them what I really feel? They probably think we see eye to eye, but that is not the case, and for the rest of that day I feel angry, depressed, and terribly lonely. I have to change whether I like it or not."

5. "I have five math classes a day. If God is on my side, I may have one student in each class who catches on quickly and is a joy to have. The others are uninterested or dense or both. Something, that still, small voice, tells me that I am wrong in blaming the students, that I am copping out, that I have to change the way I am teaching."

6. "I have taught in this school for fifteen years. The children we get today are the opposite of the eager beavers that used to live in this neighborhood. When things changed, I vowed *I* was going to change what and how I taught. And I haven't. Was that a mistake? Should I have changed in some ways? I know I should have made more of an effort

to get to know the children and their parents. Is it possible that a part of me has rejected them because they are so different from what I am and from what children and their parents used to be? Should I change? Can I change? Do I really want to change? *Something* has to change."

The type, strength, seriousness, and frequency of internal pressures will vary from teacher to teacher. These and other internal pressures are very difficult for teachers to verbalize. Verbalizing such internal pressures is hard for any person in any profession in which sustained, intimate relationships are an obvious feature. It is my opinion—substantiated by research studies—that these pressures are inherent in the nature of such work, albeit they can be exacerbated by differences among teachers in temperament, sense of security, and capacity for self-scrutiny. If they are inherent in the nature of such work, they are not necessarily negative but can be viewed as internal conflicts that can stimulate change and growth. They can have untoward effects if they are unheeded, if they do not stimulate reflection, if they lead the person to wallow in self-depreciation or apathy. Developing as a person and professional is rough stuff, especially in a world like ours, where it is too easy to feel that one is a snowflake in a storm.

Undoubtedly there will be people who will conclude that I am doing a pretty good job dissuading young people from choosing teaching as a career. To such people I can only say that in my experience what I have been saying is no more or less true than for most people in the human service professions. And leaving aside those professions, everything I have said is true in spades for the "profession of parenthood." It is no way my intention to dissuade anyone from choosing teaching as a career.

It is my intention to alert such people to the predictable realities of life in that profession. To suggest that growing up in the profession means traversing a well-paved, well-lit, pothole-free highway containing no barriers, detours, or dangers is insulting to and derogating of the capacity of young people to handle truths fateful for their lives. And if it is not insulting and derogating, it comes perilously close to asking them to renew their belief in Santa Claus.

Let us turn to examples of external pressures.

1. Undoubtedly you will hear your instructors say something about how you should think and act in response to a particular problem or event in the classroom, and your spontaneous, internal response is that you disagree; that is, it does not square with your personal experience or values. Or it may be that what the instructor is suggesting is inimical to your personal style of relating to people.

2. It will also happen in the course of your professional education that you will be observed interacting with students in the classroom and the observer (supervisor) is critical of how you handle situations. That will certainly happen when you do your practice teaching and your supervising "master" teacher presents you with a list of "don'ts and should nots," some of which you agree with and some of which you clearly do not.

3. In your first year of teaching, you will be told—formally and informally, directly or indirectly—that "this is the way we do things in this school." This may be told to you simply as information but not infrequently as a response to something you did that you thought appropriate but that "others" obviously did not.

4. Your principal or curriculum supervisor observes you in the classroom and is critical of how you handle teaching this or that subject matter. Or it may be that they disapprove of how you have organized the classroom; that is, the physical arrangement, atmosphere, "noise level." These criticisms may or may not be presented to you graciously. The important point is that you disagree with the basis of the criticism, which you regard as counterproductive or even antieducational.

5. It has been decided by the administration of the school system or the school principal that your school will be a university research site to improve the educational outcomes of the students in your school. This will require you to participate in workshops aimed at changing the substance and mode of classroom teaching, which, of course, includes *you*. You not only resent not having had a voice in the decision, but when you are in the first workshop, it is clear that you will be expected to change your accustomed ways of teaching, and these are changes about which you have a good deal of reservation.

Please note that in regard to neither internal nor external pressures have I indicated whether you or anyone else was "right or wrong."* My goal was to indicate that there will be frequent sources of pressure to change how you think and act. And implied in that goal is what I consider to be a fact: none of us takes

* There is one exception (point 5 in external pressures), and that concerns resenting not having been consulted about being selected as a research site. I am of the conviction, as I think you should be, that you should have a voice in any decision that will affect you, your students, and the school. Let us assume that the research effort is virtuous and/or justified in every respect. The fact remains that that in no way justifies ignoring the

kindly to change, because to conclude that you should change indicates something faulty in your previous thinking and action.

There was a period in my life when I spent hours working psychotherapeutically with people with personal problems. With few exceptions, they came because of habits, thoughts, feelings, and actions that produced conflicts within themselves or with others or (almost always) both. They concluded they needed help to change. It is in no way to deny the sincerity of that need to say what every psychotherapist learns (usually the hard way): at the same time that we seek change there is a part of us that mightily resists change. It makes no difference whether the need derives from internal or external pressures or both. We resist change. If that is true for people who seek change, it is even more true for people who do not seek change but are pressured by external circumstances to change.

By what criteria should we judge whether to accept or reject pressure for change? That question should be preceded by another question: To what extent do you believe that you have cornered the market on truth about how to think and act? (That, I should hasten to add, is no less relevant for those pressuring you to change than it is for you.) Have you "bought" the unverbalized invalid assumption that for any one problem or task, there is only *one* way to think and act in regard to it? Relevant here is a famous study by Dr. Max Wertheimer, who was one of the great psychologists of this century. He observed the teaching of geometry in a classroom; more specifically, how to solve the parallelogram problem. After he finished his observations, he

political principle that if you are to be affected by an educational decision, *you* should have *some* role in the decision-making process. *That is no less true for your relationship with your students.* Unilaterally made decisions have a way of engendering self-defeating consequences.

endeavored to demonstrate to the students a different way of arriving at a solution. The students not only resisted his mode of proof but asserted that he was "wrong" because the teacher had demonstrated the "right" way of proceeding. We can assume that it was not the intention of the teacher to persuade the students that for any problem in geometry there was one and only one way of demonstrating a proof. But there is no question that the students had "learned" to resist possibilities no less valid than the one they had been taught.

Nothing in what I have said was intended in any way to suggest that because you are confronted with internal or external pressure to change, you should embrace that change. What I have been implying and now make explicit is that you regard such pressure in two ways. The first is that you regard your emotional reaction, your resistance, as both an opportunity and a trap: an opportunity because the pressure may be a basis for new, productive experience, and a trap because you may too easily conclude that you do not need such an experience. You are familiar with the saying of that great American philosopher, Pogo, that "we have met the enemy and it is us." The pressure to change brings out the best and the worst in us. The second way you should regard such pressure for change is to steel yourself to ask and reflect on this question: *Independent* of my feelings, what are the pros and cons of the *substance* of the pressure; that is, what are the pedagogical pros and cons? There are always pros and cons, there are always intended and unintended consequences. Someone once said that it is hard to be completely wrong, and so if you find yourself quickly dismissing the change because it is wrong, completely wrong, it should be a warning that your resistance to change is swamping your ability dispassionately to analyze pros and cons.

In the course of your professional education and career, you will, you should, experience strong pressure to change. That is a given, whether you are an educator, a physician, a psychologist, or anyone else. It is also a given that such pressures are unsettling, sources of fear, inadequacy, and even anger. So what else is new?

What do we mean when we say "you should be true to yourself"? What that question assumes is that indeed we know ourselves: what we believe, what we stand for, what we think is and should be the relationship between our goals and the means we employ to achieve those goals. What we learn, and have repeatedly to learn, is that the pressure to change causes us to question how well we know ourselves; the pressure challenges the way we have viewed ourselves. There is no easy way out, unless you believe that how you think and act is the only way you should think and act. To be true to yourself means many things, but at its core it means being true *with* yourself; that is, accepting the fact that like every other human being your obligation to yourself is to try to make sense about *whether* you should resolve the struggle between what you are and have been, on the one hand, and what pressures for change ask you to become, on the other hand.

I would be both irresponsible and unfair if I did not indicate that the pressure for change too frequently is in an atmosphere defeating of the goals of change. Let me illustrate that point by recounting what happened in the late fifties and sixties when reformers introduced the "new math" into our schools. What you need to know is that introducing the new math was preceded by and associated with severe criticism of how teachers taught math. The pressure on teachers to change was enormous. And those pressures were external, not internal, to teachers. I ask you to perform an act of faith and accept the position that there was much to criticize. What you should not accept is the implication that what was wrong about the teaching of math was "willed" by teachers; that is, they knew better but chose not to act otherwise. No one needed to tell teachers that teaching math was not a rewarding, productive experience for them or their students. Teachers taught the way they had been taught in their school years and in their preparatory programs.

So we had an atmosphere that, if it was not intended to be unsympathetic to teachers, nevertheless produced an atmosphere not calculated to reduce the resistance of teachers to change. The new math was new, very different from the old math. That meant that teachers had to learn the new math. So what happened in many school districts is that teachers were required to attend a one- or two-week workshop in the summer before school opened when the new curriculum was to be used. I sat in on several of those workshops. It was quite an upsetting experience for me, the teachers, and those running the workshops. What became immediately apparent was that there were two sources of pressure. The first I already have mentioned: throughout the society, there was articulated criticism of our schools, especially of teachers. The second pressure that pervaded the workshops was *the pressure of time.* Teachers *had* to learn the new math *quickly*; that is, according to a time perspective I can only characterize as unforgivably stupid. *Teachers not only had to learn a new way of thinking, but they had to unlearn old ways, and to do that learning and unlearning—and with all the struggle that implies—quickly.* The frustration, fear, and resentment of the teachers were visible and almost palpable. I think it fair to say that most teachers came to these workshops with a relatively open mind, curious and even eager for new experience.

Predictably, the introduction of the new math was one of this century's major educational disasters.

This brief anecdote illustrates several themes in this book. The first is that when teachers were teaching the old math, they were ignoring *their* experiences with math when they were in school. Put more generally, they (the usual exceptions aside) were not using personal experience that would allow them to distinguish between productive and rote learning. The second theme is that teachers had passively resigned themselves to a role not connected at all to educational decision making that would affect them and their students. Teachers permitted themselves to be *objects* of change, not *participants* in decisions about change. And the third theme is that there was a lack of collegiality among teachers that would have permitted them to be whistleblowers; that is, to say about the workshops, "This is crazy, unfair, and self-defeating. We are not and cannot be ready by the opening of the new school year."

In the abstract, the rationale for the new math had many virtues. It was very far from being completely wrong! It was the rationale for implementation that was very close to being completely wrong. It was a rationale that not only created an atmosphere inimical to change but also led to workshop sessions in which the teachers of the teachers seemed to make every pedagogical-psychological mistake for which teachers have ever been criticized. One of the unfortunate consequences of this is that teachers ended up in strong disagreement with *all* of the rationale for the new math rather than distinguishing between the rationale and the mode of implementation. It was a case of throwing the baby out with the bath water.

The pressure for change, whether internal or external in

source, should never be seen apart from the atmosphere for change. In my experience, teachers too readily blame "atmosphere," which becomes an excuse for not changing. But it is also my experience that when a teacher or group of teachers comes to the conclusion that change is necessary, action is required, they can alter the atmosphere for change. Yes, the atmosphere conducive to change can be a mammoth obstacle, but that does not necessarily mean that you are without means to change it in some way. I have witnessed such change not only in schools but in a variety of complicated organizations, public and private. That is a point deserving of emphasis, because what I have said about teachers in schools is *not* peculiar to schools. I urge you to disabuse yourself of the belief that schools are unique in their social, organizational, hierarchical, decision-making features. Schools *are* different. They are *not* unique.

UNDERSTANDING CHILDREN AND THE SELF-FULFILLING PROPHECY

i do not have to convince you that today women see themselves and are seen by men in dramatically different ways than ever before. The reasons are many: that is, cultural, historical, religious, political. *But none of these factors would have produced attitudinal change if, when given opportunities, women had not demonstrated their effectiveness in new roles.* Yes, women fought for new opportunities, they gained them, but if they had not proved their competence, the social story would have been quite different than it is. Put more generally, our society was *forced* (not too strong a word) to understand women in new ways; that is, they were more capable than "we" had thought.

Let me suggest, as in the case of women, that your understanding of children is based to a serious extent on invalid assumptions and unwitting prejudice. If that is true, you are in no way different from the general public and many in the educational community. That may sound unfair and harsh, but that is not my intention. My purpose rather was simply—and I do mean simply—to suggest that you (all of us) should examine the ways in which you think about the capabilities of young people, if only because how we think about them was not in our heads when we were born. We learned how to think about them in direct and indirect ways characteristic of our society at a particular time. Indeed, I would argue that if asked to indicate the sources of how we think about children, you (we) would have a hard time responding.

For obvious reasons, my suggestion is especially relevant to anyone contemplating a career in teaching. After all, every teacher does have a conception of what his or her students are capable of learning and doing. If I asked a second-grade teacher why she is not teaching her class the calculus, she would have valid grounds for questioning my sanity. I would not blame her if she threw me out of her classroom. If she was gracious, patient, and sought to be helpful to ignoramus me, she might say, "I have to tell you that you do not understand children and their capabilities in a realistically developmental way. You have much to learn, but you will forgive me if I do not undertake that task."

The above is by way of prologue to a story about groups of middle school children. It is a story that may cause you to reflect on how you judge the capabilities of students, in this case middle school children, average age of twelve. The whole story is told in the 1978 book *Kids Who Care* by Robert Vlahakis *and* the students of Shoreham–Wading River Middle School on Long Island in New York.* I am indebted to Vlahakis for permission to use excerpts from this remarkable book.

Let us begin with the foreword, written by Francine Silverblank of Dowling College in New York.

* Vlahakis, R., and others. *Kids Who Care.* Oakdale, N.Y.: Dowling College Press, 1978.

The notion of schooling is deeply embedded in the American experience as is the controversy over its substance and approach. And there, as Hamlet noted, is the rub. I doubt if anyone would quarrel with the idea that schools should produce responsible, humane and literate people. It's the "how" that causes the problem.

From my own point of view the key to success rests on two foundations. First, it is necessary to have an administration that is concerned with providing teachers with an emotional and intellectual climate which encourages optimal learning conditions in the classroom. This means, among other things, shared decision-making. Where there is an administrative climate that sustains, encourages, and provides opportunities for shared decision-making success is more probable because the program reflects the values, experiences, and expertise of those who developed it.

Secondly, the classroom should be a community in which students learn how to learn—learn to discover concepts, principles and generalizations that can be applied, through problem-solving, to the real problems of our civilization which defy the separation of "subject" approaches by their very complex nature. Knowledge, as Dewey noted, is external; knowing is internal. Certainly it is easier to be a disciple than an inquirer, but should not the schooling process be an active one in which students take an interest in their education, take responsibility for their learning, and consciously use knowledge to solve problems and understand relationships? I think so.

This book reflects such a philosophy. It is an exciting and touching story of one teacher and his class and has much to say to all of us.

Dr. Francine Silverblank
Associate Professor of Education
Dowling College

And now let us listen to Vlahakis's introductory chapter:

This is the story of a two-year project that took place in the Shoreham–Wading River Middle School.

It's a story about a group of children who worked for close to 5,000 hours with residents at the Port Jefferson Nursing Home and Health Related Facility.

The following six sentences are the beginning of an essay written by 12-year-old Robert Caskie. It seems like the most appropriate way to begin the story:

When I first walked into the building, I felt an urge to live. I felt I was doing something that would help somebody.

After that first day, I felt very sad in some ways and very happy in others. I knew that from that day on I would never be the same.

It is the seventh time there and already I feel very happy with my work. The nursing home is a place to learn about life, love and death.

It all started out to be a simple ten-week community service project. But during that time, I found out how much my students really cared about the people they visited and how wrong it would be to stop the project. So I decided to let them continue with their volunteer work until they no longer cared.

It's been two years since then and those children will be moving on to the high school next year, so I won't be able to work with them anymore. And during these two years they've never stopped caring.

I don't know who has learned the most from this project, and I guess that it's really not important. But I do know that I've learned a lot from my own students. They've made me completely change my own attitudes and feelings toward an important part of our society— the elderly.

I've also learned something else; kids can really act as mature and responsible adults in certain kinds of situations. I found that the kids, when given a meaningful reason to behave in a responsible way, do just that. As a result of this experience, my teaching style has changed too.

The most important part of this story is the actual writings of the children. My own words are meant to tie pieces together and to explain and analyze the two years. In the children's writings, you will see how much they cared and how much they learned.

General Philosophy and Setting Up

It was a faculty meeting on April 6, 1975 that probably had the greatest influence in actually moving me toward a careful look at, analysis of, and re-structuring of my goals and methods.

The topic that we had to think about that day was *Process vs. Subject Matter.* My principal, Dr. Dennis Littky, asked us to look carefully at what we'd done over the year and ask ourselves several questions:

1. Why did we do what we did?
2. What was important about what we did?
3. What were our goals during the year?
4. Did we meet those goals by what we did?

As I sat in a corner of the library thinking over the year, I realized how far away I was from really doing what I wanted to do. The involvement of students in meaningful and important activities wasn't happening on an ongoing basis—just in bits and pieces. I began to explore what I really wanted to do and came up with the following thoughts.

Let me start with goals and work backwards. To determine my goals, I first had to decide what I thought was important, what it was that I wanted my students to gain from spending ten months in my classroom. I knew that two things were especially important to me:

1. I wanted my students to experience responsibility—to understand and live that responsibility in everything they did and be aware of their responsibility in all types of situations.
2. I also wanted my students to understand and realize that all people have separate and different

identities and feelings, that each person is a unique individual and this uniqueness is to be respected. This meant that kids would recognize that being different was not bad; it also meant that the kids would develop the ability to listen to and understand others' opinions and feelings, and to accept another's attitudes for what they are.

By teaching subject matter only, my goals were unattainable. Values clarification was probably the closest I had come to reaching those goals. However, values clarification, like much subject matter, did not seem to carry over beyond the classroom. It appeared that most things done inside the classroom were looked at by kids as "classroom" activities that were not related to real life. For example, I have seen kids involved in the classroom study of pollution and when taken on a trip to the beach to "observe" the pollution and garbage first hand absent-mindedly throw gum wrappers and candy bar wrappers on the ground. Why? This frustrated me and reinforced my feelings that something was wrong with the teaching process if no connection was made between in-school learning and out-of-school living. This was true not only for the topic of pollution but for values clarification as well. Kids discussed values clarification in the classroom and then proceeded to be uncaring and disrespectful to fellow students.

To reach my goals, I saw only one real possibility—to have the students involved in meaningful real-life experiences on a continuous basis throughout the entire school year. A month-long project is valuable, but less valuable if the child returns back to the world of the classroom and into an "unreal" situation again. I needed to find a series of experiences, through the year, that tied together, could be explored, discussed, lived and re-lived, analyzed and, finally, understood by the child so that it had a very definite and positive effect on his or her daily life.

I began to think of what would be an "ideal" situation for my class to participate in for a ten-month school year. Briefly, my plans took the following form:

SEPTEMBER: *Get Acquainted Month.* I begin to analyze the skills, attitudes and behavior of each student. We spend a lot of time getting to know each other. Creative writings and values clarification exercises are used to allow each child to express himself or herself.

OCTOBER–DECEMBER: *Real-life Experience #1.* Kids are involved in a community service experience, working at a local nursing home, two days a week for one hour.

JANUARY: *Rest and Recovery.* The nursing home experience is an emotional one and this break gives the children the opportunity for slow withdrawal before they begin another project.

FEBRUARY–MARCH: *Grandparents Class.* A group of older people from the community (could actually be the kids' grandparents) become members of the class three days a week for five weeks. These adults are responsible for all the work the students are responsible for—readings, writings and projects. The emphasis is on small, mixed groups, working together on meaningful projects.

MARCH–APRIL: *Children Teach Children.* After a two-week break, there is a five-week session during which the kids would work with the kindergarten classes in the district. They would be tutors and teach math or writing and read stories to the younger students.

MAY–JUNE: *Outdoor Education.* Students study "real" issues in the "real" environment.

I then focused on the nursing home aspect of the school year. I felt that this would be the heart of what I wanted kids involved in, and be the natural starting place.

My principal was very encouraging and motivated me to continue thinking, re-thinking, and writing about my ideas. As I look back, I realize the importance of administrative support for a teacher. Communications with other teachers have taught me that too many good ideas are wasted because of inattentive, disinterested, or unimaginative administrators. Indeed, the prodding and supportive pushing of our principal is the main reason why the Shoreham–Wading River Middle School is so outstanding. An excellent school does not consist of good teachers alone; rather what is needed is a team of good teachers, good administrators and good staff, working hand-in-hand for the benefit of the kids.

I was told to contact the community service coordinator, Winnie Pardo. She had set up a program during the year that involved our students in various community activities for certain blocks of time. The program was a good one but it did not involve any teachers with whole classes. It was voluntary on the part of the kids. I wanted a program that would be mandatory for my entire class, a part of their normal classroom experience.

Winnie and I had an exciting meeting that started me thinking about the next year. We looked at different possibilities in scheduling and activities.

We shared our thoughts with the assistant principal at the Shoreham–Wading River Middle School, Jane Wittlock, and she became involved and helped brainstorm with us, offering more ideas and her support. It began to look as though I could put my ideas into practice, and my excitement grew.

Winnie and I decided to meet for two full days during the summer to hammer out details and structure the program in order to begin it in September. We concentrated on the core of the program which was the nursing home volunteer work. To implement the program some prerequisites were necessary. The program had to function in a structured, yet informal atmosphere. Complete cooperation, discussion and preparation were needed by the two parties involved: the Shoreham–Wading River Middle School and the Port Jefferson Nursing Home and Health Related Facility.

Further, several steps had to occur in the classroom before the students could begin their work at the nursing home. The following was planned:

1. Students would read and discuss *Pigman* by Paul Zindel. This book deals with the relationship between two junior high students and an old man who befriends them.
2. Students would write essays about their grandparents, concentrating on their relationship with them, and their feelings towards them.
3. A film strip, *The Ending*, would be viewed and discussed by students.
4. Another film strip, a two-part series, *Our Elders*, would be viewed by students who would then take notes and meet in small groups to discuss the series.
5. A community service sound-slide presentation from the previous year, which had actual pictures of our own Middle School students working at nursing homes, day care centers, and nursery schools, would also be shown to the students.
6. Mike Kobel, administrator and recreation director of the nursing home, would come and speak to the students for about forty-five minutes about the nursing home, the people, the staff, and what kids could expect.
7. A touring visit to the nursing home would be arranged so that students could meet the staff and become familiar with the physical set-up of the home.

Perhaps the most difficult thing for a teacher to handle in such a project is the evaluation process. How are the kids to be graded for their work? For me, the important criterion was how well the child met his or her responsibilities. I decided to clearly outline the responsibilities and present them to the children at the beginning of the program.

Any violation of the following would be considered a failure to meet responsibilities.

Responsibilities

1. Each child knows what group(s) he is in.
2. Each child knows his/her group leader.
3. Each child knows when the bus leaves and from where. If a child misses the bus, (s)he must report to the science teacher. Discipline would come later.
4. Each child must have his/her notebook every class period and at every visit to the nursing home.
5. Each child must have a pen at all times.
6. Each child must take notes whenever there is a speaker connected with the project (nutritionist, psychologist).
7. Each child must write in his/her notebook (journal style) after every visit to the nursing home.
8. Each child must speak into a tape recorder on the bus home. These transcripts would be typed up and used as discussion material.
9. Each child must take along his/her books for the class period following the nursing home visit.

Outside of this structure, the kids were free to do what they felt comfortable doing. For each child, this turned out to be a different thing. Thus, each day at the nursing home, there were twenty-five children having twenty-five different experiences, each one unique and personal to that child.

When the program became operational, I found that I had to keep a running track on each child to see if the basic responsibilities, as outlined, were met. For example, if John forgot his notebook on a day that he was going to listen to the nutritionist, that was equal to failing a test. As far as I was concerned, he had failed to meet his responsibilities.

Interestingly enough, all of the children were able to handle their responsibilities well. There were three minor violations during the first week, but once the kids saw how serious I was, they became responsible people.

I credit much of the success of the program to the fact that the kids knew very clearly what was expected of them in advance. It was rewarding for me to see that they could handle responsibility when it was defined for them [pp. 1-7].

Here are a couple of other excerpts from the book:

One of my responsibilities was to "educate" the nursing home staff about what could and should be discussed with our kids. The staff were professionals in their area and did an excellent job. However, when it came to dealing with kids I considered myself the best judge of what the kids could handle and what the kids could deal with; and, in short, I tried to turn the staff on to dealing with kids on the kids' own terms.

We broke the class into groups of eight or nine and each group had a staff member from our school and a nursing home staff member. I thought that this supervised situation would help things run smoothly and give students the security they needed.

The residents at the nursing home were enthusiastic and thrilled to see the kids. The kids, on their part, were prepared, attentive, and very involved. They were very excited and soon began talking about "project time," when they would make gifts for Christmas so that every resident in the nursing home would have a present.

Curriculum-wise, the nursing home visits generated many questions. During discussions, the kids poured out innumerable feelings, observations, and analyses. I had always been weak at holding discussions in class—it was hard to keep everyone's attention and get everybody involved. It was just the opposite now. The interest, which stemmed from the kids' actual experience, was enough stimulation and motivation for the kids to be attentive. They listened and wanted to know the answers—it was their problems they were dealing with. I tried to raise as few issues as possible; generally I pointed out an issue from the transcripts which, again, was something they said and could relate to. By just letting the discussions go, the kids related their experiences, got involved and came out of their shells; they shared their experiences with each other. I was incredibly impressed with the way that the children listened to each other discuss their personal experiences.

The discussions were documented by me and became my curriculum. It was difficult to measure the value of these discussions, but I knew they were important because they answered many questions, concerns, and fears that the children had.

I discussed evaluation with the students—grading! How would I grade this project? I was not giving any formal tests on the nursing home, but they were being tested nonetheless. How responsible were they? Did they have their notebooks, pen? Did they write in their journals? Were they where they were supposed to be? Were they involved? Those were important guidelines.

Another point is also worth noting; I told the children that if they forgot their notebooks three times, then they would be dismissed from the project. In reality, if that problem arose, I do not know how I would have dealt with it—if it meant actual removal from the project. However, in their minds, the kids understood and accepted this, and did not forget any of their responsibilities [pp. 10–11].

On Wednesday, November 19th, I invited all the parents to school to explain the program to them in detail. The class began to prepare for Parents' Night by brainstorming on what we wanted to do that night. I told them it would be very easy for me to speak to parents and present the program to them, but I did not feel that would be right. I wanted the kids to be involved since it was their project.

We spent an entire class period trying to figure out what would be the most effective way to get parents to understand the program. It became very important for each child to make sure that someone in his family showed up. Due to the flexible schedule, I was able to meet with kids for four class periods on Monday and then for the entire school day on Tuesday, so we could prepare for Wednesday.

On Tuesday, the principal spent four hours with the class, helping out, running small groups, producing material for the next evening. From 8:40 AM until 2:25 PM we all devoted our energies to that evening. That single day was an incredible experience in itself—spending all that time together, everyone working on the same task.

We produced a booklet for that evening. The booklet contained three sets of transcripts, some excerpts I had chosen from kids' journals and at least one essay from each child involved.

The evening began with me talking about the program for about 25 minutes. I explained how and why it started, the rationale for and the philosophy of the program, the structure of the program and the variety of experiences available to students.

Next, the parents split into two groups. One group had the assignment of reading at least ten essays from the students' booklet and then writing five "I learned . . ." statements. The other group worked with the kids in an activity called *Sharing Trios.* There were two children and one adult in each group. Each person had to talk for one minute while the other two listened. The children had to talk about their nursing home experience. The adults had to support each child positively. We kept switching groups for about twenty minutes, until each adult had the opportunity to hear several children discuss their experiences.

Every parent was involved in both group situations; by the end of the evening they had read about, listened to, and understood the program. Before the parents left, I showed a twelve-minute slide-tape presentation—another opportunity to hear the students and see their work.

Dr. Littky concluded the evening by reading several of the "I learned . . ." statements to the group. I nearly cried as he read statements that the parents had written—statements that hit at many of the things I was trying to get at—statements that I interpreted as support for the program, for the school, and for myself [pp. 18–19].

In my experience, at least, most people (including teachers and administrators) react with surprise to such a story. Years ago, I visited the Shoreham–Wading River Middle School, where that and similar projects were being implemented. Following that and another visit, I took advantage of numerous opportunities to ask parent and teacher groups how they would feel about Vlahakis's project; that is, presenting it as a "what if" fantasy. *I never told them that such a project was being successfully implemented.* It would take a separate chapter to describe the list of objections people raised. With one exception (to be noted later), the objections were based on a conception of twelve-year-olds that said such children should and could not assume and discharge the responsibilities asked of them. In addition, it would be psychologically upsetting to place such children in a nursing home, where the plight of its residents is all too visible. Furthermore, there was no way that parents in their right minds would or should permit their children to engage in such a project. When I would then tell them that my "what if" fantasy was a reality, they found it hard to believe. And matters were not helped any when I would go on to say that Vlahakis's project was not unique. Indeed, I knew and had read about many similar projects around the country. Granted that the absolute number of such projects is far from large, especially in middle schools, their significance goes way beyond numbers. Their significance inheres in the challenge they present to our accustomed, overlearned way of viewing the capabilities of people.

We are all in one or another way victims of a way of thinking called *the self-fulfilling prophecy*: you start with assumptions about the capabilities of this or that labeled group, you react to that group as if the assumptions were God-given, indisputable facts, and, of course, you end up "proving" you are "right." We do not take kindly to challenges to our assumptions about the capabilities of people. Indeed, one way of looking at human history is as a succession of self-fulfilling prophecies that were never articulated or overcome except through struggle, more often than not bloody struggle.

You come to your professional education with unchallenged assumptions, and you will also be exposed to the assumptions held by others, for example, your instructors, supervisors. That says nothing derogatory about you or others. You are part of the human fraternity-sorority! What it does say is that you should have the moral and intellectual obligation and courage to examine your assumptions, *especially when you find yourself reacting strongly and negatively to challenges to those assumptions.* Your reactions may be "right." They *may* also be "wrong." That is what is meant by trying to lead an *examined* life. To go through life, whether in its personal or professional aspects, unable to examine dearly held assumptions may not be a fate worse than death, but it comes perilously close.

Now to the exception I alluded to earlier. A very frequent response to the "what if" fantasy came from teachers. It went like this: "The atmosphere and traditions of my school would never permit me to think seriously about doing such a project. To do what Mr. Vlahakis did requires a supportive administration, not one that tells you to do your thing only in a classroom." That objection is valid but incomplete. Of course such projects require the support of the principal and other administrators. But initially it requires a teacher who wants to do such a project. I have witnessed several instances where the principal encouraged such projects but no teacher came forward with one. Clearly, what is required at a minimum is a teacher and principal willing to implement such a project. That was true in the Shoreham–Wading River Middle School. Vlahakis wanted to do the project, and Dennis Littky, the principal, was more than eager for him to do it. It goes without saying that the atmosphere at that school was (in my experience) unique in the way it encouraged and permitted everyone to articulate and challenge assumptions on which rested conceptions of what students were capable of and what a school can be. It was not a case of *anything* goes. It was a case of where a thought-through, carefully planned and supervised "what if" could get a hearing and support.

The number of Dennis Littkys is, unfortunately, not large. But that is no excuse for teachers passively to resign themselves to the way things are. One of the themes I have emphasized in previous chapters is that teachers *as a group* do have power, potential and actual, to influence policies and practices. If I have emphasized that theme, it is not only because that exercise of power can benefit students but, no less importantly, because of what it means for the personal-intellectual-professional growth of teachers. *Unless the conditions of such growth exist for teachers, they cannot create and sustain such conditions for students.* To achieve such conditions for teachers and students is, in my opinion, the most important issue confronting American education. That explains why I have written this book: in the next couple of decades, the needed changes in American education will not come about unless those who will enter the profession are better prepared to meet challenges to the dynamics of the self-fulfilling prophecy.

Another objection to the story of Shoreham–Wading River goes like this: That school was in an affluent community in which highly educated and education-conscious parents were unusually supportive of educational change. What if a Dennis Littky was principal in a school in a poor, blue-collar community where education, let alone a transformed education, was neither prized nor supported, materially or otherwise? And what if the school in which he became principal was a disorganized, disorganizing place to which the police frequently were called?

The answers to these questions can be found in two places. The first is *Doc. The Story of Dennis Littky and His Fight for a Better School*, a book written by Susan Kammeraad-Campbell in 1989, published by Contemporary Books. The second is a two-hour movie (*A Town Torn Apart*) based on the book and nationally televised by NBC on November 30, 1992. The book is engrossing. The movie I found absolutely stirring. Knowing Littky as well and as long as I do, and what TV movies do to truth, I was prepared for the movie to contain numerous distortions and irrelevances and, like too many classrooms, to make the interesting uninteresting. It is a superb film demonstrating what a principal *and* teachers can do to undo self-fulfilling prophecies. It is the best film I have ever seen on the differences between teaching children and teaching subject matter. Anyone contemplating a career in education should, must, see this film. It is the best argument in favor of teaching as an exciting profession.

chapter 11

THE "NONREADING"
PROFESSIONAL

*I*n a book like this it is hard to avoid sermonizing. In this final chapter I consciously and deliberately will sermonize.

In the case of teachers, one hopes that they never give up trying to "save lives," regardless of how long they have been teaching. In my case, a very obvious senior citizen, I still seek to save the lives of those entering the educational profession! Let us leave aside the thorny question of which criteria we should employ to judge whether we have "saved" the life of a professional. But there is one criterion about which I feel so strongly, and about which there is general agreement, that it deserves a sermon! Unfortunately, despite such agreement in the abstract, it is a criterion honored more in the breach than in the practice— one of the preconditions for giving a sermon. Sermons tell us what we already know we should think and do; the purpose of the sermon is to remind us that we have fallen short of the mark and we should try to do better.

A prefatory note of caution. What I say in this chapter is not peculiar to those in education. There is no evidence to suggest that educational practitioners are dramatically different from other practitioners in their failure to read the literature in their fields; that is, to *want* to know what others are thinking and writing because they feel they *need* to know in order to have the sense that they are intellectually-professionally alive and enlarging their horizons. It is really irrelevant to my purposes whether educators are more or less "nonreaders" than those in other professions. In my experience, too many practitioners in education have little interest in reading what others are thinking and writing in regard to issues in the field.

How many times have you heard educators and others bemoan the fact that most students look upon books as uninteresting, unimportant, and irrelevant to their lives? How many times have you heard that one of the adverse consequences of TV is that reading books (or even the newspaper) has been further eroded as a source of intellectual pleasure? Are we not dismayed (too weak a word) when we are told about studies demonstrating that young people's knowledge of the world they live in is scandalously poor? And are we not taken aback (again too weak a phrase) when we learn that they are *uninterested* in that world? It is irrelevant whether the results of these studies are no different or worse than what studies from the most distant past may have indicated. As one researcher said to me, "Anyone who takes comfort in the argument that this is the way it has always been has learned nothing from history." It was the same researcher who went on to say, "How many people know that the founding fathers who gave us our wondrous Constitution were, as a group, the most voracious readers of the history of the issues with which they were confronted, more voracious than any comparable group in human history?" Let me interrupt this sermon with a story.

Back in the sixties, I invited a friend to talk to my colleagues and graduate students. Edward Cohart was a physician and an internationally respected epidemiologist. The point of his talk was in the form of a question: Why is it that in the United States the treatment of choice for breast cancer in women is radical mastectomy, while in England surgeons opt for lumpectomy, a much less invasive and pervasive procedure? The difference between the two countries, he said, was so striking as to suggest that one of them had to be "wrong"; that is, the psychological and bodily consequences of the two approaches for women were too obvious to permit one to justify either as the dominant procedure. He then went on to compare the results in both countries in terms of longevity, morbidity, and other indices of outcomes. The most cautious conclusion the comparisons permitted was that there were *no* differences in outcomes. A less cautious but still justified conclusion was that the outcomes favored lumpectomy. Both conclusions obviously should have caused the medical community in the United States to ponder the frequency with which it resorted to radical mastectomy. But it did not! Not in the mid sixties, when Cohart gave his talk. It took two or more decades before American surgeons began to reduce the frequency of radical mastectomy as the surgery of choice.

How do we explain this? One partial answer is that it is an instance of the way people resist changing highly overlearned ways of thinking and acting, even when the "objective" evidence suggests that a change in viewpoint is in order. American surgeons were trained to believe that radical mastectomy was the procedure of choice. They learned that from their teachers, and they learned it well. (Obviously, that is the risk you run whether you are in medical school or in a teacher preparatory program!)

But there is another part of the answer, and it has to do with reading. Of course, there were some American surgeons who had read the British studies, but it was apparently the case that most surgeons had not read them. Among practicing surgeons (as among practitioners in other professions), the number who read, really read, the literature in their field is not large. I understand the argument that the demands made on professionals (for example, physicians and teachers) are so great, so persistent, so energy draining as to make serious reading in their fields at best a luxury and at worst an unpleasant bore. But to understand all is not to forgive all! It is my opinion that if more physicians had read the British studies, it might have spurred more of them to rethink their practices. In recent years, there has been a steady increase in the United States in lumpectomies. If more surgeons had earlier read and digested the impact of those studies, that increase might have started long before it did. The important point here is that practitioners in diverse professions read very little in their fields. I cannot cite studies to prove that assertion. All I can say is that whenever I have talked with leading people in this or that profession, one of their complaints is that the "everyday" practitioner does not read, does not keep up with new research findings, new ideas. As one such leader said, "They are in a rut, withering on the vine, and don't know it. What bothers me more than not reading in the field—that I can understand up to a point—is that too many of them are *uninterested* in reading."

This problem has been so general and worrisome as to cause professional organizations *and* state legislatures to *require* educational and medical practitioners to take more courses or attend workshops. I italicize *require* because it confirms what has long been obvious: too many practitioners do not read what they should be reading. I have nothing against continuing education, but I have to confess that I am not impressed with what some people (adults and children) learn when learning is mandated, when it is not internally dictated and sought. I have attended and given workshops, and I have heard and given scores more lectures in continuing education programs. Audiences, I have concluded, comprise two groups: those who are there because they want to be there, and those who are there because they are required or expected to be there. I may be accused of undue pessimism when I say that the number in the latter group exceeds the number in the former.

My wife is an avid attendee at workshops, and I tag along, dutifully and reluctantly. Rarely have I regretted attending. Workshops can be stimulating. They have an important role to play, especially if they not only spur you to reflection about how you think and act but also to stimulate you to read more extensively about the issues. Being a passive but interested listener to someone giving you his or her version of truth is one thing; actively seeking to read, analyze, and digest what different people have written about a particular idea or practice is quite another thing. Truth has many versions.

Let us take an example from the educational arena. Almost twenty years ago, the federal government commissioned an extensive study to evaluate the outcomes of federal efforts to improve education. It is a landmark study (in several volumes!). There are two ways you can respond to the study. One is with discouragement because the outcomes were far from favorable. The other is with encouragement because one of the few clear findings was that favorable outcomes were associated with schools where teachers and administrators (and frequently parents) cooperatively planned and implemented actions for change; that is, the proposals for change were themselves outcomes of intellectual-professional discussions reflective of a collegiality making for commitment on the part of all participants. That was a very important finding, the significance of which cannot be overestimated, flying, as it does, in the face of the "traditional" way proposals for change originate and are implemented in our schools. That is not only my opinion but that of others who read the study. If there were people who read the study, how do I explain the sad fact that among the many scores of teachers I asked, *none* had read the study and only a handful had even "heard" about it? Before you scapegoat teachers, you should know that *none* of them had ever been exposed to that study in their preparatory programs. Having said that, however, I have to point out that the study received a good deal of play in professional journals, weeklies, newspapers, and newsletters. Even if the teachers with whom I spoke had not been told about the study in their preparatory programs, it is not unfair to say that there were numerous opportunities for them to become aware of that study. But only if they felt the obligation to read what was going on in the field. Not to feel such an obligation is, I must in all candor say, inexcusable. A professional person is, among other things, someone whose responsibilities include knowing what others in the field think, do, and have found and reported. *If you knew that your physician, or lawyer, or tax accountant read next to nothing in his or her field, would you not consider finding someone else to whom to bring your problems?* In recent years, there has been a dramatic escalation in the number of malpractice suits against physicians. That escalation has several valid and invalid sources, but let us not forget that one basis for a malpractice suit is that the person did not know something he or she *should* have known; that is, if the person had read what he or she should have been reading in the *normal* course of professional living, that person should have acted otherwise. A professional person is not one who stopped reading after finishing formal training. Reading is more than desirable, it is crucial. If I were czar of education, I would seek to stimulate and support the professionals in each school to devote at least one hour each week to a meeting in which is discussed a published study, report, or book that everyone had read beforehand. Professionals should always be "going to school."

You should read articles and books the way you listen to your instructors: carefully, respectfully, but critically. Because someone says something or has written something does not mean that you should accept it. In listening or reading, you have two tasks or, better yet, obligations. The first is to seek to understand the rationale; that is, to understand it in terms of the writer's experience and his or her use of formal studies and the experiences of others that are the basis for the rationale. Put another way, you should seek to comprehend "where the person is coming from." It may surprise you when I say that this kind of reading is not easy, especially when what we are reading is unfamiliar or clearly discrepant with our way of thinking and practicing. When we read something that challenges our accustomed ways, our internal resistances to change come to the fore and can interfere with even a semidispassionate comprehension of the writer's argument. I speak here from personal experience. Reading for the purpose of truly comprehending another person's way of thinking and acting is the opposite of a routine practice. It is hard. We do not take kindly to new ideas. By not reading, of course, you eliminate that difficulty, but at the expense of your intellectual-personal-professional development.

The flip side of the problem is no less dangerous: uncritically accepting what you read (or you hear in lectures) as gospel.

Because a "voice of authority" has said or written something does not mean that you should accept it. Such voices have what we call a "demand characteristic"; that is, "If Professor or writer X says Y, the message is that I should believe it and do it." I am reminded here of a medical colleague who was one of the greats in radiology. One of the first things he would do with a new cohort of interns was to present them with x-rays of several people, ask them to study them, and then to give their opinions about what the x-rays revealed. The interns would unfailingly come up with lists of pathologies. After all, if Professor Henry Kaplan, *the* Professor Kaplan, asked them to study the x-rays, something was amiss in those patients. The interns were, to say the least, chagrined to learn that the x-rays were those of normal people. It was their first lesson about how easy it is, how dangerous it is, to see what you think a voice of authority says you should see. It is a lesson no less valid for reading than for seeing.

I am not advocating reading for pleasure. Reading for the express purpose of enlarging your intellectual-personal horizons is hard work, a struggle, precisely because that kind of reading requires you to walk that fine line between uncritical acceptance and premature dismissal of new ideas. The pleasure from such reading comes when you can say that you have engaged in a struggle, you have tried to be fair to yourself and the writer, and you can justify the resolution of the struggle on grounds other than habit, sheer feeling, or prejudice.

We are living in times when education and educators—in our public schools, colleges, and universities—are subject to all kinds of criticism and pressure to change. The issues are many, complicated, fateful, and they will not go away. The day is past when anyone entering *any* human service profession can remain ignorant of those issues, the different positions taken, and their implications for action. How these issues get played out will depend on many factors, predictable and unpredictable. But certainly one of those factors will be the outlook, knowledge, creativity, and courage of those who will enter these professions. In the case of our public schools, a major factor will be those who become teachers. You can react to that prediction as a problem or an opportunity. Obviously, I regard it as an opportunity for those who seek to understand themselves, their students, and the society in which we live. No longer can a teacher's horizons be circumscribed by a classroom, or a school, or a school system. It has *never* been the case that schools were impervious to societal forces and dynamics. But up until the post–World War II era, our schools acted as if they were truly oases walled off from their surrounding. That is no longer possible. World War II, like all other major wars in human history, ushered in societal changes that changed everybody and everything. Indeed, the crisis in education today inheres in the fact that educators have to deal with those larger social forces, like it or not. Some have not liked it. For them, it is a problem, not an opportunity requiring change, adaptation, innovation, and understanding. For those who see it as an opportunity, the challenge is both formidable and exciting. It is not the kind of challenge appropriate for those who see the classroom as a retreat from the larger society. And it is not the kind of challenge for those content to let others— in and outside of schools—decide how teachers should think and act. I am not suggesting that teachers go it alone, that there are not other voices that should be heard in decision making. What I am asserting is that teachers have to become sophisticated about several things: the allocation and uses of power, the processes of decision making, the role and uses of community groups and resources, the nature and consequences of the legislative process, the history of the educational crisis with which we are confronted, and the sources of the diverse conflicting rationales about the goals of education. In the course of your professional preparation, you will be exposed to some of these things, although not as much as you should be (in my opinion). In any event, however adequate or inadequate that preparation may be, you should feel obliged to assume the responsibility to become and remain knowledgeable about what is happening in your field. There is no one way to accomplish that. Reading is one of the best ways. *Your* professional "salvation" will not come from outside of yourself. A professional is someone who has something *to profess.* Your obligation to yourself and your profession is to know what is going on; that is, what others are experiencing, studying, and writing. Teaching need not be, must not be, a lonely profession. Reading is one of the better prescriptions for diluting the sense of intellectual-professional isolation as well as the sense that you stopped developing. No profession more than education provides as exciting an opportunity to understand the society in which we live: how it has changed, will change, should change. Will there be problems, frustrations, ups and downs, second thoughts, even despair? Of course. Is personal, intellectual, professional "growing up" easy? Of course not. End of sermon!